VERACRUZ ALL NATURAL

REYNA AND MARITZA VÁZQUEZ
WITH NILS BERNSTEIN

VERACRUZ ALL NATURAL

FRESH MEXICAN RECIPES FROM OUR AMERICAN HOME

SIMON ELEMENT

NEW YORK   AMSTERDAM/ANTWERP   LONDON
TORONTO   SYDNEY/MELBOURNE   NEW DELHI

SIMON
ELEMENT

An Imprint of Simon & Schuster, LLC
1230 Avenue of the Americas
New York, NY 10020

First Simon Element hardcover edition June 2026

SIMON ELEMENT is a registered trademark of Simon & Schuster, LLC

Simon & Schuster strongly believes in freedom of expression and stands against censorship in all its forms. For more information, visit BooksBelong.com.

For information about special discounts for bulk purchases, please contact Simon & Schuster Special Sales at 1-866-506-1949 or business@simonandschuster.com.

The Simon & Schuster Speakers Bureau can bring authors to your live event. For more information or to book an event, contact the Simon & Schuster Speakers Bureau at 1-866-248-3049 or visit our website at www.simonspeakers.com.

Interior design by Robert Diaz
Photography by Mackenzie Smith

Manufactured in China

1 3 5 7 9 10 8 6 4 2

The Library of Congress Cataloging-in-Publication data has been applied for.

ISBN 978-1-6680-5035-4
ISBN 978-1-6680-5036-1 (ebook)

 Let's stay in touch! Scan here to get book recommendations, exclusive offers, and more delivered to your inbox.

THIS BOOK IS
DEDICATED TO OUR
MOM, REYNA GUTIÉRREZ,
AND TO VERACRUZ
ALL NATURAL

CONTENTS

CHAPTER 3
BREAKFAST ALL NATURAL—AND ALL DAY 100

CHAPTER 4
COMFORT SOUPS AND STEWS 116

CHAPTER 5
VEGETABLES IN THE MIDDLE OF THE PLATE 140

CHAPTER 6
FROM THE VERACRUZ SEA 164

INTRODUCTION

OUR STORY

GROWING UP IN VERACRUZ, MEXICO, we had entrepreneurship in our blood. Both our mom and dad were business owners, and their drive shaped us. Mama Reyna ran a restaurant out of our tiny home, turning our living space into a bustling hub of activity. By the time we were eight, we could knead masa, blend aguas frescas, chop vegetables, and run to the chicken store on the corner without a second thought. While other kids played with Easy-Bake Ovens, we were baking makeshift cakes in old tuna cans over a fire in the backyard. We were resourceful and creative, and knew hard work and its value. The lessons stayed with us long after the flames of those backyard fires died down.

A few years before we moved to the United States, Maritza and I started working together selling encyclopedias in small villages across the state of Veracruz, along Mexico's eastern coast. At dawn, our aunt would pick us up in her brown van, packed tight with stacks of books we had to sell that day. The team—my aunt and her partner, two other sales boys, and us—squeezed in the little space left, our knees bumping against one another as we set off. Before we arrived at the first village, we'd make a quick stop to grab something to eat. A tamal or atole (a corn-based drink) was always the perfect choice—filling enough to calm our stomachs for the hours ahead.

Once we arrived, our aunt would hand each of us three heavy books and a handful of contracts for customers who wanted to set up payment plans. We walked the quiet streets of each pueblito, knocking door-to-door hoping to make a sale. When hunger struck again, we'd convene at the local tortillería to buy a kilo of fresh, hot tortillas, then to a corner store to pick up fresh cheese and pickled jalapeños. That was always the best part of the day, sitting together, laughing, eating, and savoring the simple joy of being young and in one another's company. The tacos of crumbly queso fresco softening against the warm tortillas and spiked with jalapeños were all the more delicious because of—not despite—their simplicity. Those days were our first taste of life beyond our home kitchen, a chance to explore the world of sales and customer relationships. We may not have known it then, but we were learning lessons about food, business, and community far beyond what was written in the encyclopedias we carried.

Around the same time, our older brother Armando was in college, Maritza had finished high school, and we found ourselves asking, *what now?* The gap between our reality and that of other social classes became even more apparent when Armando began his studies and made friends with people from very different means. Seeing the opportunities that a college education could provide planted a seed in him—a desire to find a better life, not just for himself, but for all of us.

As we transitioned into adulthood, the weight of responsibility grew heavier, both for us and for our parents. It became clear that it was time for us to start taking care of ourselves. In our community, it was common for girls to begin searching for a boyfriend or even a husband by the age of fifteen, someone who could support them as they started a family. But that wasn't the life we wanted. Maritza dreamed of continuing her education beyond high school, though sadly the financial strain was simply too much for our family. Even finishing high school had been a sacrifice, and once she had done so, Maritza chose to set aside her dreams to help support our family—a decision made out of necessity.

Armando was the first of us to leave for Austin, Texas, joining an uncle and aunt who were already living there. Before long, our dad followed. Armando was a driving force in our family's decision to relocate: He always had a clear vision and an unwavering ambition to change the course of our lives. Once he arrived in the United States, Armando focused on working hard and saving every dollar he could. Every week, at the same time, he would call us. To get the call, we'd walk to a neighbor's house on the corner of the street, which was our only telephone access. For about thirty minutes, Armando would describe his new life: the safety and peace of his surroundings, the green trees, a beautiful lake where families gathered to spend time together. His words painted a picture of a place so different from what we knew. When our dad joined him, the two of them sent home whatever money they could save.

Armando never stopped trying to convince our mom to reunite the family, and after many conversations, we knew our departure was inevitable. Looking back now, we're forever grateful to him for being the spark of our new life. But at the time, we didn't feel that way. The thought of leaving behind everything familiar was overwhelming, even with the promise of a better future.

Reyna: *One afternoon in the spring of 1999, when I was sixteen, my mother pulled me aside in our little dirt-floored home and told me we would be leaving in the morning. She said it was our only hope for better opportunities. All I heard was that I was*

Maritza at a
school dance in
Veracruz, 1987

leaving my friends and extended family behind. Maritza had chosen to stay with our grandma for the time being. My mom didn't tell me what to expect, or how risky it was to cross the border, because she wanted me to feel hopeful, not scared. I knew deep inside that she was worried and in my mind the shock outweighed whatever optimism my mother wanted me to embrace.

We left the next morning. I was dressed in black jeans and my best blouse, a shiny one not really fit for traveling. We had packed a few changes of clothes and personal hygiene items in a backpack and headed to the bus that would take us and other immigrants to the border between Mexico and Texas. We would cross the Rio Grande on foot. I don't remember much of the bus trip, but I do recall arriving in Piedras Negras, a Mexican border town about two and a half hours from San Antonio.

The plan was to wait until our coyote gave the signal to cross the Rio Grande. He handed us a plastic bag and we stripped to our underwear and placed the clothes we had been wearing in the bag to keep them dry. He then told us we had to leave everything behind to not look suspicious walking with backpacks. I remember feeling devastated when I was forced to leave my little photo album on the riverbank. It had a white plastic cover, and its pages were filled with snapshots of my life: my school dances, my best friends, a picture of me in my beige quinceañera dress and a tiny wallet-size photo of my dear cousin Rosi. That worn, precious picture was the only thing I managed to save. I slipped it into my hair bun, desperate to keep it dry and safe. It was my last tangible connection to the life I had left behind.

The call to start the crossing came and the coyote insisted that my mom and I cross separately, but my mom refused, understanding the dangers of traveling alone as a young girl. Together, we huddled on one inflatable tube that plunged into the cold, rushing waters of the Rio Grande by daylight and someone pushed us across to the other shore.

Our first meal in the United States happened the next day at a McDonald's in San Antonio, and it felt like an introduction to a completely new world. We'd never eaten burgers and fries before. While fast-food chains existed in Veracruz, they were considered a luxury compared to street food or my mom's home cooking. Our second meal was a burrito, which was just as foreign to me as McDonald's—it wasn't something people ate in Veracruz, or in most parts of Mexico, for that matter. We arrived in Austin late at night, disoriented and unsure of the time. But I'll never forget my awe as I took in the clean streets and the bright lights of downtown.

The buildings seemed to sparkle, and the sight was unlike anything I had ever seen. It was a moment that marked the beginning of an entirely new chapter in our lives.

Maritza: *Meanwhile, I stayed behind in Mexico. I had met somebody who had been selling encyclopedias with us and I decided to remain with our grandmother. A few months later, my boyfriend chose to go north as well. I was just eighteen years old and wanted to "do things correctly," so I married him. One week later, we set out on the same route my sister and my mom had taken. My mother-in-law escorted us on a bus to the border. Once there, we rented a hotel room and tried to make sense of the process, though we had little information. Strangers approached us offering guidance and we didn't know whom to trust. An older woman stood out: She had a warmth that put us at ease, and in that moment, she seemed like the best option to help us.*

The next evening, we met the woman at a house that felt like a makeshift hostel. Inside, beds of every kind—bunk beds, singles, and mats on the floor—were crammed into every corner. It wasn't a permanent residence; people came and went, waiting for their chance to cross. The house was crowded with people lying on the floor, standing, or sitting—some with companions, others alone. The uncertainty of what came next was suffocating.

We were there for only a few hours, though it felt like days. Suddenly, the phone rang. The call had come—it was time. At 9 p.m. we left the house. We had to put the clothes we were wearing in plastic bags and cross in our underwear. It was October, and the night was cold and dark when our group of about fifteen people reached the edge of the river.

We had no inflatable tubes and no assistance, and I didn't know how to swim. Anxiously, I told my fear to the man leading the group. He gathered everyone and instructed them to stay close to me. "You just go to the other side of the river." Then he added. "If someone stays behind, there's nothing we can do." As we entered the water, the group dispersed. The current was strong, and I was alone. The farther I waded into the river, the harder it became to touch the bottom. The current pulled at me and dragged me away. I desperately tried to keep my head above water, but I was feeling my strength leaving me. Finally, I screamed for my husband who was nearing the US shore. For a moment, he hesitated, torn between safety and the sound of my voice, then, he threw himself into the water, swimming back to me. Reaching beneath the surface, he grasped my arm and pulled me forward. We fought the current and made it to the other side.

2010: We put out our first "palapa," and it was actually the strongest day of sales we'd ever had. This day was the turning point of our success.

Once across, we found a hollow in the ground—perhaps carved by the river—where we quickly changed into the dry clothes we had carried in the small plastic bags. The chill of the night was biting as we dressed, but there was no time to rest. We were instructed to walk. For what felt like an hour, we hiked through thick brush with thorny bushes scratching our legs, until we reached a highway. There, we waited for about thirty minutes. My body ached from the cold and exhaustion. The next set of instructions came: We had to run fast and without stopping into a neighborhood where there was a particular house. By the time we finally arrived, it was early morning. The house was empty of furniture and crowded with people who looked like they'd been there for days. Some were injured, others looked sick, and the air was thick with the smell of sweat. We spent a day and night in that place, without food, and eventually, we were told to pile into an SUV. The driver tried to separate me from my husband, insisting that I board the first vehicle, but we refused and waited for the next ride together. Hours later, we arrived in Austin.

I have a clear memory of looking up at the sky and seeing the clouds lined with the rays of the rising sun. I felt a wave of relief: We made it! Then, almost immediately, the anxiety crept back up, the uncertainty of a new life just beginning.

We lived with our father and brother in a three-bedroom apartment in East Austin. To us, it already felt like a huge step up. For the first time, we had hot water, a solid floor, heating and air conditioning, and a real kitchen with appliances. There was even a washer and dryer—and a pool! These were luxuries we had never known, and we were grateful.

But with those comforts came new challenges. Though our mother had always taught us to be independent and self-sufficient, life as young female immigrants in Austin was anything but easy. It was terrifying to even leave the apartment, not knowing if we might be stopped by authorities and what the consequences could be. While we had been taught English in school, we had never actually used it in real life. Meeting people, finding work, and contributing to our new community all felt out of reach because of the language barrier. In many ways, our brother took on the role of our father after he moved to the US. He guided us as best he could, helping us navigate this unfamiliar world.

We were both hired as servers at the same Mexican restaurant, and we worked hard to save every penny while our mother found

work cleaning houses. The job was an adjustment in every sense. Communicating with customers was challenging, and the food we served was confusing. We'd rarely eaten flour tortillas in Mexico, and the nachos, liquid cheese, overstuffed burritos, and enchiladas drowned in red gravy were completely foreign to us. Whether the menu was labeled Tex-Mex or simply Mexican, it was a far cry from the vegetable- and seafood-based dishes we'd grown up eating. Still, we pushed through. Those early days were a whirlwind of adapting to a new culture, learning on the job, and finding our place in this new world. We wanted to thrive—not just survive—and every step we took, no matter how small, brought us closer to that dream.

In Austin, almost everything felt foreign, but we discovered one comforting truth: We could still find Mexican ingredients. Re-creating some of our favorite dishes from home became a way to stay connected to the culture and traditions we had left behind. Certain ingredients central to our cooking were surprisingly expensive or difficult to source, but we managed to create family meals that reminded us of our Sunday dinners in Veracruz. Those meals brought us a sense of belonging in a place that still felt unfamiliar.

As we became more comfortable with our surroundings, we started to notice something important. The food we missed most—the fresh, wholesome, vibrant dishes of Veracruz—was nearly impossible to find here. It wasn't just the flavors but the way this food made us feel: nourished, energized, and comforted.

That realization sparked an idea. What if we could introduce the food of Veracruz to our new community? We had a hunch that Austin, with its blend of health-conscious, outdoorsy, and adventurous eaters, would embrace the fresh, nutritious, and flavorful meals we had grown up eating. We soon realized we had identified a niche—one that combined health and comfort in a way that felt authentic to us. With that, we began developing a menu inspired by the food of our childhood, a menu we were excited to share with our new neighbors. It wasn't just about cooking; it was about creating a bridge between two worlds, bringing the heart of Veracruz to Austin's table.

Of course, the American Dream isn't something that's just handed over. The country is built on the contributions of immigrants, especially when it comes to the culinary world, yet despite the value that immigrant communities bring, there are few pathways to obtain legal residency. Without the proper papers at the time, we had no access to public assistance, bank loans, or even bank accounts. Everyone told us it was impossible to open a business without documents, that we would never be able to make it. But our mother had always taught us that dreams without action are just fantasies. So, despite the odds, we were determined to make it work.

We had a million reasons to keep pushing, but none was more powerful than our desire to relieve our mother. By the time we were settling in the US, she was battling health issues. We couldn't bear the thought of her continuing to clean houses. We wanted to unburden her and give her the life she deserved— a life where she wouldn't have to work so hard just to get by.

2011: Damian, Maritza's son, loved playing while helping us. It kept him entertained while we worked long shifts, since we couldn't afford a babysitter.

Our business began in a small trailer tucked away in a corner of César Chávez Street, adjacent to downtown on the east side. We were fortunate to have a generous friend, Rania, who rented us space in the parking lot of her convenience store, El Aguacate, for almost nothing. The lot was small, just spacious enough for us to assemble fruit cups and prepare smoothies, aguas frescas, and Mexican snow cones, known as raspados. We offered flavors like tamarind, watermelon, pineapple, peach, and coconut—flavors that were new to Austin at the time.

Reyna: *The trailer was originally designed for raspados, and it came with the necessary freezer equipment. In front of the trailer, we had two small tables, but even that wasn't enough to catch the attention of passing drivers, despite our efforts to wave them in. We were open from 7 a.m. to 9 p.m., and on our most profitable day, we earned eighty dollars. It wasn't much, but it felt like a small victory in a sea of challenges.*

Maritza: *We made sacrifices just to keep the business afloat. We often slept in the trailer, and sometimes we would turn off utilities at home to save money. By then I was a mother and sometimes I reflect on the fact that one of my kids' earliest memories was of all the candles replacing the lights in our apartment. For him, it was a beautiful reality, a world where even the simplest things, like a flickering candle, could create a sense of warmth and magic.*

After two years of fourteen-hour days alternating working at the restaurant and in the trailer, and with the help of our mom, we were able to buy a bigger trailer, and we added tacos to the menu. That's when word began to spread. We saw that we had to offer more than snacks. The community was a patchwork of people. There was a strong Hispanic population of Chicanos and Mexicans, as well as African Americans and newly arrived artists who were attracted to the vibrant East Austin scene. Those locals were excited by what we took for granted: handmade tortillas pressed to order, unique homemade salsas like our five-chile Salsa Macha (page 81) and dairy-free Creamy Jalapeño Salsa (page 73). We had vegetarian and vegan tacos filled with roasted poblano chiles, refried beans, mushrooms, potatoes, cauliflower, carrots, greens, and avocado, because that's how we eat at home. We adapted Austin's famous breakfast migas into a portable taco version (page 106) that our busy customers could grab from the window and take on the go to work or the gym.

Over time, we realized how much we loved working together, and how our skills complemented each other perfectly. In the beginning, we handled everything, from inventory and purchasing to customer service and marketing. For three years, we worked as waitresses while simultaneously building our business. It wasn't until we sustained ourselves solely with the profit from the trailer that we could finance our own growth.

In our world, leading by example always took precedence over profits. We believed in doing things the right way, even if it meant sacrificing short-term gain. Because of this, we slowly established ourselves as one of the few female Mexican business owners at the time, navigating an industry shaped by challenges such as cultural barriers and evolving labor standards. Today, our journey has taken us much further than we ever imagined. We've grown into four food trucks, four brick-and-mortar locations, and a 130-seat sit-down restaurant. We serve thousands of guests every day, and yet every taco is still cooked to order, with handmade tortillas and homemade salsas. It's a testament to the heart and soul we've poured into this business.

In 2022, just as we were preparing to open our first full-service restaurant, Veracruz Fonda & Bar, *The New York Times* published an article about us. It said, "The Vázquez sisters have done more than serve popular tacos from a food truck. They've changed the landscape of Austin dining, paving the way for more regional Mexican offerings in a city long defined by Tex-Mex cooking, and helping other immigrants, and their families, to build restaurant groups with minimal capital." It seemed unreal. That morning, among the joy, excitement, and the showering of congratulations, it dawned on us that we had built something that had reached people outside of our city. In November 2024, we received a Michelin Bib Gourmand award.

For two girls who grew up in a one-room dirt-floor house in Veracruz, making our way to Austin in 1999 as teenagers with no resources, the accolades were remarkable. It was a gift to not just be recognized for the naturally healthful vegetable- and seafood-based cuisine of Veracruz and elsewhere in Mexico and Texas—but as role models and entrepreneurs.

In Reyna's home kitchen—our mother, Reyna Gutiérrez; Reyna Vázquez; and Maritza Vázquez.

OUR FOOD

A LONG, NARROW CRESCENT ON Mexico's eastern side, the state of Veracruz is historically a major entrance point for people from Europe and Africa. These influences shine through in our cuisine. For example, African influences inspire stews thickened with peanuts and root vegetables. Rice and seafood are infused with coconut, and we often use plantains, tamarind, hibiscus, and sesame seeds—all ingredients found in food from West Africa and the Caribbean. European cuisine inspires dishes like our famous pescado a la Veracruzana, a dish that features two ingredients that don't appear "Mexican": olives and capers. These ingredients also show up in our stews (estofados) along with almonds and raisins. Arroz a la tumbada, a saucy rice dish, could easily be seen as a close cousin to Spanish paella.

Indigenous Mexican traditions remain strong, too, shining through in vegan stews of beans, seeds, and chiles, salt-cured nopales (cactus paddles with the heartiness of sliced steak), and our wide variety of tamales, from giant zacahuiles (massive tamales that can serve hundreds of people) to individual ones filled with raw shrimp. These traditions evolved long before the Spanish brought most meat and dairy animals to Mexico, with protein coming primarily from beans, greens, nuts, and seeds.

We have now lived in Texas for more than twenty-five years, which is longer than we lived in Mexico, and so our food has evolved. We will always feel connected to the flavors of Veracruz and southern Mexico, but we have been influenced by Austin, too. The Southern American diet was a novelty for us, and we had to adapt to what our customers needed. We've aimed to be inclusive from the beginning.

We didn't realize it at the time, but the "cuisine" that we grew up with, despite our having little money, was rich, varied, healthy, and delicious. Our small bodies were fueled primarily by queso fresco, beans, and tortillas. We never ate much red meat, and it still plays a minor role in our diets today compared to other proteins like shrimp, chicken, and eggs. Meat was reserved for special occasions. In its place, we usually used bones, chicken feet, pig feet, buche (pork stomach), and basically whatever the butcher would clean off the good cuts of meat. He knew my mom would ask for the "cat food" and he knew what she meant. My mom had to be creative with her tiny budget and would use the worst pieces and transform them into main dishes fortified with vegetables or rice—and a really good salsa, of course. That was the magic of her cooking.

Shrimp and other shellfish were inexpensive everywhere in Veracruz, and we put them in soups and stews. The shells flavored the broth. We had a fisherman uncle who would bring us fat and flaky red snapper (huachinango), slender but meaty snook or sea bass (robalo), tender mojarra (a type of tilapia), and buttery pámpano. These are the building blocks of our cooking today.

Veracruz's varied climate and geography make for a produce-rich region. Our counters were stocked with sturdy vegetables like ripe plantains, chayote (a firm summer squash), nopales, cauliflower, mushrooms, and all kinds of potatoes and sweet potatoes. Our corn was earthy, chewy and savory, not like the sugary sweet corn that's popular in the US. Easy techniques—like charring vegetables and using powerfully flavored herbs, spices, and chiles—help give our dishes a deeper flavor than they would have if we simply cooked meat in a sauce. Our food is still vegetable-heavy, which resonates with our local customers and is adaptable to many diets.

When we call our food "all natural," this is what we're talking about: We start with vegetables and fruit harvested at their peak. We have adapted our cooking to our busy Texas schedules dictated at first by working multiple jobs and now by running our growing business. In Veracruz we'd enjoy spending the day cooking for the family; now we rarely have the luxury of time. Luckily, growing up in a home that doubled as a restaurant taught us efficiency and the value of prepping everything in advance. These skills come in handy for our taco truck businesses, but they are also indispensable for making economical, varied, and energizing meals at home that can be pulled off on a busy weeknight.

We hope that this book inspires you to try dishes, ingredients, and techniques that may feel unusual at first but will soon become familiar and comforting. Working with masa is even easier than making pie crust, biscuits, or pancakes, because it's so forgiving. Burning ingredients (see Tatemado, page 70) is a bonus, not a mistake. Because sauces are key to so many of our dishes, it's easy to make vegetarian substitutions without compromising a dish's integrity or authenticity. Main dishes can become appetizers—or tacos the next day—and salads, sides, and veggie dishes are complex enough to make into full meals by adding rice, beans, salsa, and/or fresh tortillas. Let these recipes be inspirations and not rigid rules.

Disfruta!

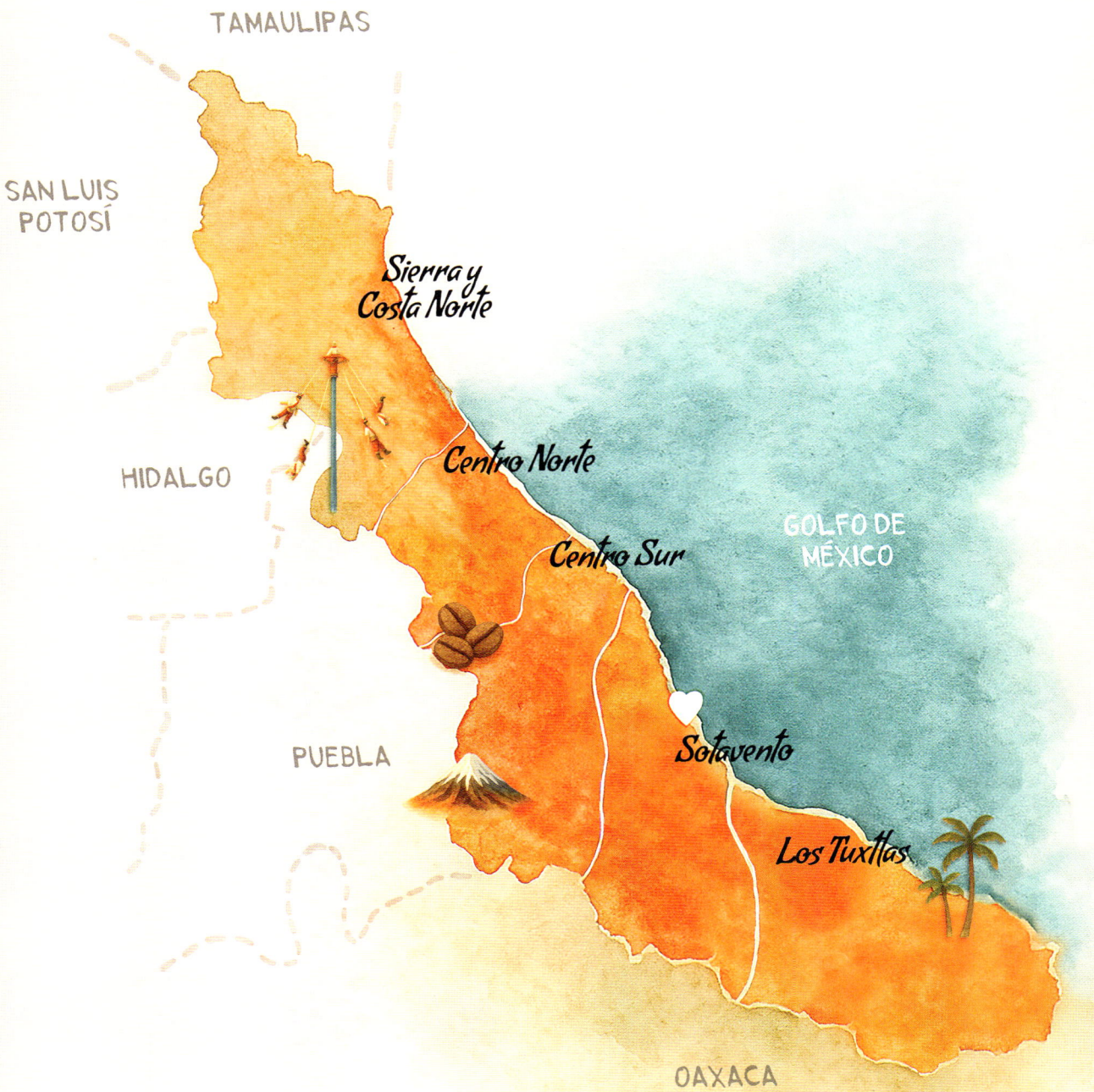

TAMAULIPAS

SAN LUIS
POTOSÍ

Sierra y
Costa Norte

HIDALGO

Centro Norte

Centro Sur

GOLFO DE
MÉXICO

PUEBLA

Sotavento

Los Tuxtlas

OAXACA

1

THE VERACRUZ ALL NATURAL PANTRY AND BASICS

"Ajo, cebolla y limón y déjate de inyección."

(GARLIC, ONION, AND LIME, AND FORGET THE INJECTION.)

This Mexican take on "an apple a day keeps the doctor away" shows how the core ingredients of Mexican cooking—garlic, onion, and lime, plus corn, beans, tomatoes, chiles, squash, and other simple ingredients—make for an exceptionally nutritious and delicious plant-rich diet full of complex carbohydrates, protein, and fiber.

This chapter offers the basic rice, bean, and broth recipes that, along with tortillas, are the building blocks for making simple and healthy meals from scratch.

A NOTE ABOUT INGREDIENTS:

Salt: We use Morton's kosher salt, and each recipe was tested with that brand. Different brands of kosher salt vary in volume and salinity. So, a teaspoon of one brand's kosher salt may not taste the same as another's. Always taste as you go—especially at the end, before serving the dish—and adjust as needed.

Oil: Our preferred cooking oil is avocado oil. It's minimally processed, with a neutral flavor and a high smoke point, meaning it can tolerate the high cooking temperatures we use without smoking. We also like to use extra-virgin olive oil, because it adds a complementary layer of flavor to most of our dishes. When shallow or deep-frying, any neutral cooking oil can be used if cost is an issue.

Onions: We use white onions because that's what we used in Mexico. Their relatively mild flavor and low sulfur content make them especially refreshing when used raw or quickly charred. Red onions can be a good substitute, because they also have a low sulfur content, making them less pungent when raw. Yellow onions are not the best substitute, though, because they're pungent and sulfurous, and turn sweet and complex only when cooked for a long time. Fun fact: If you're only used to cooking with yellow onions, you might be surprised that cutting white onions is much easier on your eyes.

Mexican crema: Like sour cream and crème fraîche, Mexican crema is a cultured cream that's comparable in composition to sour cream but a little less sour and thick. It is usually labeled as "crema," "crema Mexicana," or "media crema." It's available at any Mexican or Latino market and most large supermarkets. Look in the refrigerated dairy aisle (where you'd find sour cream) or the canned dairy aisle (where you'd find evaporated milk), as there are refrigerated and canned versions that can be used interchangeably. While all brands work well, we like Nestlé Media Crema in the can, which is a little looser and less salty than other brands; it's imported from Mexico but easy to find here. If we are looking for a creamy texture in a sauce, we often use coconut milk and/or Greek yogurt in place of some of the cream, which makes the sauce a bit lighter and more complex.

A NOTE ABOUT EQUIPMENT AND HEAT:

A **tortilla press** is a must for making your own corn tortillas. (There are other ways to roll or pat out corn tortillas, but tortilla presses are ubiquitous because they do a far better job than any other tool.) They are affordable and easy to find online or in Mexican groceries.

We grind small quantities of chiles, garlic, and spices in a **molcajete**, a Mexican mortar and pestle made of volcanic stone that has a coarser texture than other mortars and pestles, which is ideal for grinding tough dried chiles, vegetable skins, and hard spices. If you don't have a molcajete, use a blender (if the quantity is sufficient to keep the mixture moving in the blades) or a small but powerful food processor.

Other than that, no special equipment is needed to make the recipes in this book (though a blender is recommended). A **comal**—a Mexican griddle usually made of steel or cast iron—is great for cooking tortillas and many other dishes, but any large, flat, heavy griddle pan will work. We tend to use heavy pans—such as a cast iron—and high heat to cook the majority of our dishes. In general, when cooking in oil, we heat cast-iron pans dry for at least 2 minutes, then add oil, then the ingredients. The oil should be sizzling hot when the first ingredient is added.

A NOTE ABOUT TIMING:

Each recipes's estimated time assumes that the ingredients are already prepped (onions chopped, chiles stemmed and seeded, etc.). As a rule of thumb, it's always good to have all ingredients and equipment ready to go before you start cooking.

TORTILLAS

¡PERO PRIMERO, MASA! (But first, masa!)
Because corn tortillas are—literally and
metaphorically—our bread and butter, masa
is the cornerstone of our cooking. Masa is
the dough used to make corn tortillas and
countless other snacks such as picadas,
gorditas, and tamales.

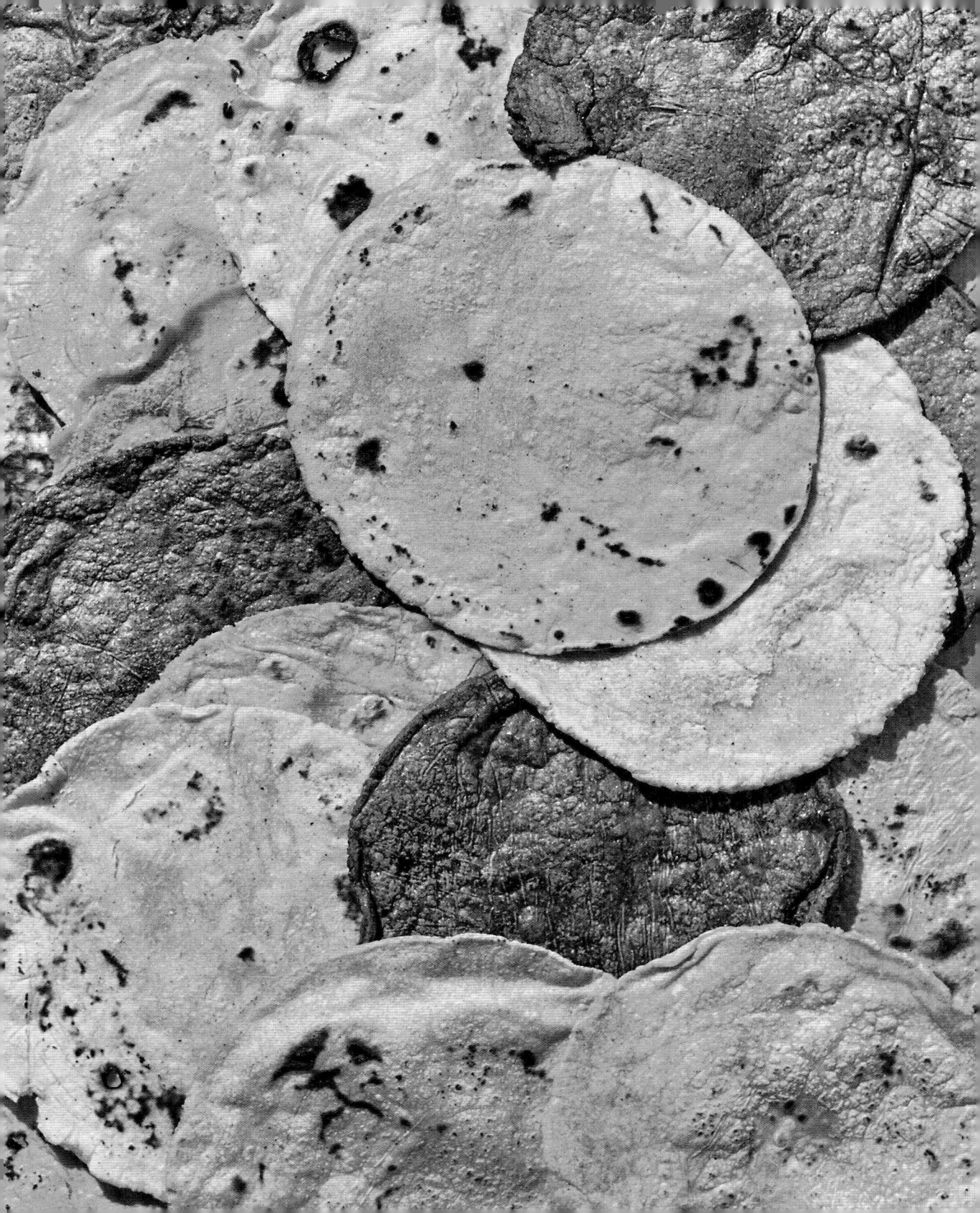

MASA IS MADE WHEN dried field corn is nixtamalized—soaked in a calcium hydroxide solution to improve flavor and nutrition and give it a workable texture—and then ground into a dough. This dough is masa fresca, or fresh masa. When it's dried and ground into a flour (so it can be stored and rehydrated into a dough with some water), it's called masa harina. In either case, the only ingredients are corn and calcium hydroxide.

You can sometimes find fresh masa from a tortillería that nixtamalizes its own corn, but fresh masa has a short shelf life, and using masa harina lets you have masa any time you want—and that means making tortillas yourself. We still make tortillas fresh to order at all of our locations, and it's always been something that helps us stand out. We recommend you do the same, except in chilaquiles (see page 109) and migas (see pages 105 and 106), where store-bought tortillas work well. There are many brands of masa harina, including some like Masienda that use heirloom corn from small producers. We usually use Maseca brand (in US stores, the label says "instant corn masa flour" in English and Spanish), which is widely available. Its fine texture forms a dough that's easy to work with and makes tortillas that hold together well.

Making corn tortillas is easier than making pie crust—and harder to mess up. Just add water, press, and cook! OK, success isn't quite that instantaneous; masa is like salsa dancing, playing soccer, or cooking: It's easy to learn but hard to master. But take advantage of the "easy to learn" part and start making tortillas, gorditas, picadas, and empanadas on your own. Even your mistakes will taste great, and the sense of accomplishment will inspire you to experiment further.

Comals and Tortilla Presses

A comal is a griddle with a very low, or gently sloping, rim. Traditionally, they are made of clay, but now carbon steel or cast-iron comals are more common and more reliably effective. A cast-iron skillet or griddle—round or rectangular—works well in place of a comal. Nonstick surfaces aren't recommended because they don't make the charred flecks that give tortillas their classic look and flavor.

Like a new cast-iron pan, a new steel or iron comal should be seasoned before use (lightly oiled and baked at very high heat). After that, you shouldn't need oil to cook tortillas. In fact, one hallmark of corn tortillas, as opposed to flour tortillas, is that no fat is added to the dough.

A tortilla press is a simple tool to form evenly thin and round tortillas before laying them on your comal or griddle. Good tortilla presses are inexpensive and easy to find online or in Mexican groceries. Even though you can roll tortillas with a rolling pin, or by pressing down hard with a flat-bottomed pan or baking dish—or even with your hands, after a lifetime of experience—a press forms a perfect thin tortilla with one split-second motion, so it's worth it if you plan to make them regularly.

CORN TORTILLA DOUGH
(Masa para Tortillas)

Making homemade tortillas may seem intimidating, but after a bit of practice, you'll become a natural. And, because there's no gluten in corn masa, it's impossible to overwork the dough. It really is as simple as adding water to masa harina until you get the right texture, pressing, then cooking on a hot comal or griddle until it's done. The tortilla press does most of the work, and the dough is forgiving; if any of your tortillas fall apart, put the dough back in the bowl and start again.

In a mixing bowl, combine the masa harina and water and mix with your hands until it's a uniform dough. The texture you're looking for is like Play-Doh: It shouldn't break apart when you squeeze it, and it shouldn't stick to your hands or the bowl. If the masa is too dry, wet your hands in warm water and continue to knead until the dough is hydrated. If it sticks to your hands, you have two options: A pinch at a time, add more masa harina and knead, or spread it out, let it air-dry for a minute or so, and keep kneading. Wrap tightly with plastic wrap until ready to use. It will keep in the refrigerator for up to 2 days. Just make sure to bring it to room temperature before using.

MAKES ENOUGH DOUGH FOR 15 TORTILLAS, 12 PICADAS, OR 12 EMPANADAS

3 cups masa harina, such as Maseca brand

2 cups warm water

TOTAL COOK TIME

10 minutes

CORN TORTILLAS
(Tortillas de Maíz)

1. Form 15 equal-size balls of masa (dough) about 1½ inches in diameter, depending on the size of your tortilla press. Keep the balls covered at all times, but if they dry out on the outside, just knead them again before pressing.

2. Heat a dry comal, griddle, or large skillet over medium heat. Press each dough ball on a tortilla press between two pieces of plastic (a split ziplock bag works well), press hard, peel the plastic away, and carefully lay the raw tortilla flat on the hot pan.

3. After about 30 seconds, when the tortilla is no longer sticking to the surface of the pan, flip it to cook the other side for another 30 seconds, then flip it back on the first side for a final 30 seconds, at which point it should puff up. This means you've made a perfect tortilla. If it doesn't puff up, don't worry, it will still taste good! The next time, after the second flip, gently press with your hand or a balled-up towel, which encourages the puff.

4. Pull each tortilla from the heat when it's speckled with dark spots but still pliable. Stack the tortillas as you cook them, and cover with a dry dish towel. Their residual heat will keep the tortillas hot and soft. Serve hot.

MAKES 15 TORTILLAS

1 recipe Corn Tortilla Dough (page 38)

TOTAL COOK TIME

1 hour

Reheating Corn Tortillas

The best way to reheat room-temperature corn tortillas is simply to return them to a hot, dry griddle for about 20 seconds per side. For larger quantities of homemade or store-bought tortillas that have been refrigerated, there are two methods:

Microwave: Wrap a stack of no more than 12 tortillas in a lightly damp dish towel and microwave until the ones in the middle are hot (start with 60 seconds, and then 30-second intervals). Let the tortillas sit for 2 minutes before serving.

Oven: Wrap a stack of no more than 12 tortillas in a damp dish towel, then wrap with aluminum foil and place them in a 350°F oven for 10 minutes.

PICADAS

Picadas are essentially just thick, sturdy tortillas with a pinched rim to hold toppings, but unlike tortillas, they constitute a dish unto themselves. There are versions of these all over Mexico, where they're sometimes called picaditas, pellizcadas, memelas, memelitas, or garnachas. They are even more forgiving than tortillas and are a great introduction to working with masa. Like tostadas, they are the perfect base for any topping you want.

1. Form 12 equal-size balls of masa (dough) about 2 inches in diameter (as you become comfortable making picadas, feel free to make them any size you like). Press each dough ball lightly to make a disk that is thicker than a tortilla (about $1/8$ inch thick). Because picadas don't have to be flattened as firmly as thin tortillas (which the tortilla press facilitates), you can press them using a heavy flat-bottomed object like a baking pan or skillet, but a tortilla press is easiest.

2. Heat a dry comal, griddle, or large skillet over medium heat. Press each dough ball between two pieces of plastic (a split ziplock bag works well), peel the plastic away, and carefully lay the raw picada flat on the hot griddle.

3. After about 45 seconds, when the picada is no longer sticking to the surface of the pan, flip it to cook the other side for another 45 seconds, then flip it back on the first side for a final 45 seconds. The timing might vary, and it won't puff up like a tortilla, but the finished picada should be pliable and speckled with dark brown spots.

4. After each picada is removed from the comal, immediately use your fingers to shape it: With your thumb pressing down on the edge, work your way around the picada using your pointer finger of the same hand to squeeze some dough from near the middle of the picada toward your thumb to form a rim. Stack the picadas as you cook and form them.

5. When ready to serve, place the picadas back on the warm griddle to heat through before topping, 1 to 2 minutes per side. It's important that the picadas themselves are hot when you serve them, which is why they benefit from a final pass on the comal after being pinched and topped.

MAKES 12 PICADAS

1 recipe Corn Tortilla Dough (page 38), made with 1 teaspoon kosher salt dissolved into the water before mixing

TOTAL COOK TIME

1 hour

NOTE

Picada toppings can be as simple as salsa and queso or, really, anything you crave: Think beans, eggs, guacamole, onion, cilantro, avocado. Meat or vegetables are optional here, but they will, of course, bring your picadas from a simple antojito (small dish) to full meal status.

EMPANADAS

For us, an empanada is simply corn tortilla dough that has been folded around any filling and cooked with the filling already inside. They can be baked in an oven or cooked on a comal, but we prefer the texture and flavor of empanadas fried in oil. Remember, when frying at the correct temperature (350°F to 375°F), food absorbs very little oil, and you can strain the oil through a fine-mesh strainer lined with cheesecloth and then reuse it.

1. In a large mixing bowl, whisk together the masa harina and flour. Add the water to another large bowl and dissolve the salt in it. Add to the masa harina mixture and mix with your hands until it's a uniform dough. The texture you're looking for is similar to Play-Doh: It shouldn't break apart when you squeeze it, and it shouldn't stick to your hands or the bowl. If the masa is too dry, wet your hands in warm water and continue to knead until the dough is hydrated. If it sticks to your hands, you have two options: A pinch at a time, add more masa harina and knead, or spread it out, let it air-dry for a minute or so, and keep kneading. Wrap tightly with plastic wrap until ready to use. It will keep covered in the refrigerator for up to 2 days. Just make sure to bring it to room temperature before using.

2. Form 12 equal-size balls of masa (dough) about 2 inches in diameter. Place each dough ball on a tortilla press between two pieces of plastic (a split ziplock bag works well), and press lightly to make a disk that is thicker than a tortilla (about $1/8$ inch thick and 5 inches in diameter).

3. Remove the top plastic sheet and add about $1^1/2$ tablespoons of your choice of filling to one side of the flattened dough. Using the plastic on the bottom of the dough to prevent the dough from sticking, fold the tortilla over to enclose the filling, and pinch the edges closed to make a stuffed half-moon shape. Resist the urge to stuff your empanadas to the max—if they are overfilled, the masa will break during the frying process and that's where things get messy.

4. In a deep, heavy skillet, add oil to a depth of $1/2$ inch. Heat over medium-high heat to between 350°F and 375°F, or until the corner of an empanada sizzles happily on contact. Add the empanadas in a single layer and cook for about 2 minutes per side, or until deep golden brown.

5. Drain on paper towels and serve hot or warm.

MAKES 12 EMPANADAS

3 cups masa harina, such as Maseca brand

¼ cup all-purpose flour

2 cups warm water

1 teaspoon salt

2 cups filling of your choice (grated melting cheese, chopped cooked vegetables, shredded cooked chicken, etc.)

Vegetable oil, for frying

TOTAL COOK TIME

1 hour

THROUGHOUT THE BOOK, you'll see rice as a side dish, and cooked rice used in soups and stews, inside tacos, and as a main component of dishes like our Coconut Rice with Seafood (page 172). For our recipes, we use long-grain white rice or jasmine rice.

You can certainly use whatever rice-cooking method you like, but we include our favorite basic rice recipes here because they bring a little more color and flavor than plain steamed rice. Briefly sautéing the rice before adding the cooking liquid has a few benefits: It brings out a subtly nutty flavor, helps keep the grains separate and not sticky, and results in a fluffier texture.

RICE
(Arroz)

WHITE RICE
(Arroz Blanco)

Putting a little onion, garlic, and some mixed vegetables in plain steamed rice adds nutrition, color, and flavor with hardly any extra time or effort. This is a great base for leftover veggies or a bag of precut mixed vegetables from the freezer section.

1. Set a fine-mesh strainer over a large mixing bowl and pour the rice into the strainer. Rinse and drain the rice multiple times, agitating it as needed, until the water almost runs clear. Set aside.

2. In a medium saucepan, heat the oil over medium heat. Add the onion and garlic and cook, stirring often, until fragrant and translucent, about 2 minutes. Add the rice and cook, stirring often, another 3 minutes.

3. Raise the heat to high, add the vegetables, salt, and 5 cups fresh water and bring to a boil while scraping any browned bits from the bottom. Once it boils, turn the heat down to low, cover, and cook for 10 minutes. Working quickly, lift the lid and stir the rice, then cover and cook for another 10 minutes.

4. Turn off the heat and keep the rice covered until ready to serve.

SERVES 4 TO 6

2 cups long-grain white rice

1 tablespoon extra-virgin olive oil

½ small white onion, minced

1 garlic clove, minced

½ cup mixed vegetables (e.g., carrots, corn, peas, green beans), fresh or frozen

1½ teaspoons kosher salt

TOTAL COOK TIME

45 minutes

MEXICAN RICE
(Arroz a la Mexicana)

Whereas White Rice (page 46) is a nice canvas for colorful or richly flavored sauces, reddish Mexican rice pairs well with tacos. Though we typically prefer to use fresh tomatoes in all our cooking, in this rare instance, canned tomatoes are fine and still bring plenty of flavor to this dish.

1. In a blender, add the tomatoes, onion, garlic, and salt and blend until smooth. Add enough broth to reach $4^{1}/_{4}$ cups and set aside.

2. In a medium, deep skillet or saucepan, heat the oil over medium-high heat. Add the rice and cook, stirring often, for 3 minutes.

3. Add the tomato mixture and bring to a boil, then turn the heat down to low, cover, and cook for 25 minutes, at which point all the liquid should be absorbed.

4. Turn off the heat and keep the rice covered until ready to serve.

SERVES 4 TO 6

3 Roma tomatoes

¼ medium white onion

3 garlic cloves, peeled

2 teaspoons kosher salt

2 tc 3 cups Vegetable Broth (page 55) or water

¼ cup vegetable oil

2 cups long-grain white rice, rinsed anc well drained

TOTAL COOK TIME

45 minutes

BEANS
(Frijoles)

MAKING BEANS FROM SCRATCH couldn't be easier. When you boil dried beans in water until they're soft, you have beans that are better tasting and cheaper than canned. More often than not, the beans on our stove are black beans.

BLACK BEANS
(Frijoles Negros)

1. In a stockpot or Dutch oven, add the beans, garlic, onion, salt, and 3 quarts water. Bring to a boil over high heat, then turn the heat down to medium, partly cover the pot, and cook for 90 minutes or longer, if needed, until the beans are soft enough to smash with a fork

2. Use right away or store in a tightly sealed container in their cooking liquid for up to 5 days in the refrigerator or up to 6 months in the freezer.

MAKES ABOUT 6 CUPS

1 pound dried black beans

6 garlic cloves, peeled and smashed

½ medium white onion, roughly chopped

2 teaspoons kosher salt

TOTAL COOK TIME

2 hours

REFRIED BEANS
(Frijoles Refritos)

SERVES 8

1 cup olive, avocado, or vegetable oil or pork lard

½ medium white onion, finely minced

1 recipe Black Beans (recipe above) or 6 cups canned black beans, drained and rinsed

Kosher salt, to taste

TOTAL COOK TIME

20 minutes, plus 2 hours bean cooking time

When we were growing up, we didn't have a lot of kitchen tools, so we learned to use what we had on hand. Our method of mashing warm beans with a heavy pint glass to make a creamy dish that still has some texture is quick and time-tested. Resist the urge to blend the beans in a food processor or to mash them when they are cold: They have better flavor when mashed manually, and a creamier texture when mashed hot.

Don't stress over the amount of oil in this recipe; it's what makes them so good! Canned beans work great here, too. Our favorite brand is S&W organic black beans.

1. In a large, deep cast-iron or steel skillet (not nonstick, since the surface could get damaged by the mashing process), heat the oil over medium-high heat. Add the onion and cook for 5 to 7 minutes, stirring occasionally, until it's a deep golden brown.

2. Using a slotted spoon, add the beans, and once they're warmed through, start smashing them with the bottom of a heavy glass. A combination of mashing and "smearing" the beans works best. Depending on the texture you're aiming for, add bean cooking liquid or water a few tablespoons at a time—more for creamier beans that would be served as a side, or just a bit for a bean paste, which can be used as a filling for gorditas or empanadas, or as a dip.

3. Serve immediately, or store covered in the refrigerator for up to 4 days.

BEANS WITH HOJA SANTA AND COCONUT MILK

(Frijoles con Hoja Santa y Leche de Coco)

This recipe is a must-try if you can find fresh hoja santa, an herb with giant heart-shaped leaves that's native to Mexico and especially common in Veracruz and Southern Mexico. It can often be found in Mexican groceries in the Southern US. Its intoxicating root beer–like aroma and flavor, with notes of anise and mint, add incredible complexity to a pot of beans. Coconut milk adds richness and another layer of flavor that's a little reminiscent of the combination of coconut milk and Thai basil in Thai curries. Serve with white rice, or anywhere you'd otherwise serve black beans.

Add the hoja santa and coconut milk to the hot pot of beans and cook over medium heat, stirring gently, for 5 minutes. In this short time, the leaves will have infused the liquid with flavor. Serve right away.

SERVES 8

4 fresh hoja santa leaves (see Note)

1½ cups unsweetened coconut milk

1 recipe Black Beans (page 49), freshly made

TOTAL COOK TIME

15 minutes, plus 2 hours bean cooking time

NOTE

While it has a very different flavor from hoja santa, basil is also delicious in this recipe. In place of the hoja santa, use 2 to 3 stems of basil (each with 6 to 8 large leaves).

BEAN GORDITAS
(Gorditas de Frijol)

Our mother ran a tiny restaurant out of our home in Veracruz, and these fried bean-stuffed tortillas were the most popular weekend dish. Some customers ordered them for a snack, while other people piled them on their plate for a full meal. I (Reyna) always made sure every gordita that came out was fried perfectly. It was relaxing for me, and I liked to believe that it was the reason people came to buy so many.

You can use store-bought refried beans for these in a pinch, but because the only ingredients are masa and beans, you'll ultimately want to make these with the homemade beans, as listed in the recipe, for the best flavor.

1. In a large bowl, add the masa harina, flour, salt, and warm water. Mix well with your hands until the mixture is as moist as possible without sticking to your hands. If it's too dry, add more water, and if too moist, just let it sit a few minutes before continuing to knead it. Remember, there's no gluten here, so you need not worry about overmixing.

2. Form 12 equal-size balls that are just over 2 inches in diameter. To shape the gorditas, press each ball into the palm of your hand, creating a thick-walled indent. Place a heaping tablespoon of beans in it, then close the dough around the beans to encase them completely and form again into a ball.

3. Flatten each gordita between two pieces of plastic (a split ziplock bag works well) to a thickness of between $1/8$ and $1/4$ inch (not as thin as tortillas). Be gentle with the tortilla press so that you don't press them so thin that the beans break through. Alternatively, press the masa between plastic on your countertop with a heavy flat-bottomed object like a baking pan or skillet.

4. In a deep, heavy skillet, add oil to a depth of $1/4$ inch. Heat over medium-high heat until it shimmers (it's hot enough when a tiny ball of dough sizzles and floats on contact). Cook the gorditas one by one, about 1 minute per side, or until golden and, ideally, puffed up a little. Using a spoon, baste the tops of the gorditas with oil while they cook. Drain on paper towels and serve hot.

SERVES 4 TO 6

1 pound masa harina, such as Maseca brand

5 tablespoons all-purpose flour

$2\frac{1}{2}$ teaspoons kosher salt

3 cups warm water

$1\frac{1}{2}$ cups Refried Beans (page 49), cold or at room temperature (see Note)

Vegetable oil, for frying

TOTAL COOK TIME

1 hour

NOTE

The beans should be cooked down to a thicker texture than usual, more scoopable than pourable. When cooled to room temperature or refrigerated, they will firm up even more, making the gorditas easier to form.

"NO VAYAS A TIRAR EL CALDO" translates to "don't throw the broth away." It was a favorite saying of our family's matriarchs. We come from a line of incredibly resourceful women who never failed to use everything to the last drop, and they would always conjure up some tasty soup or sauce just from the liquid leftover from cooking meat, seafood, and vegetables.

Today, we rarely rely on repurposed cooking liquid because we usually have these broths in our fridge or freezer. Having homemade broths on hand doesn't just give you better flavor without the additives of most store-bought broths, but it puts satisfying meal-worthy soups at your fingertips.

BROTH
(Caldo)

VEGETABLE BROTH
(Caldo de Verduras)

This broth has a deep vegetable flavor and is well seasoned—quite a contrast from many store-bought broths that are either too salty or completely lacking in taste. This is a handy base for soups and stews (it can stand in for chicken broth in any recipe), and it can even be sipped on its own. For an easy vegetable soup, add some diced vegetables, queso fresco, and/or fideos (see Tip, page 138), garnished with avocado, cilantro, and lime.

MAKES ABOUT 2 QUARTS

4 celery stalks, preferably with leaves, roughly chopped

3 large carrots, roughly chopped

2 medium white onions, unpeeled, roughly chopped

1 head garlic, halved crosswise to expose the cloves

1 handful fresh parsley sprigs

1 fresh rosemary sprig

1 fresh thyme sprig

1½ teaspoons kosher salt

TOTAL COOK TIME

2½ hours

1. In a large stockpot, combine the celery, carrots, onions, garlic, parsley, rosemary, thyme, and salt plus 3 quarts water. Bring to a boil over high heat, then turn the heat down to medium-low and simmer, uncovered, for 2 hours.

2. Taste the broth and if it's too reduced or salty, add more water; if it's too bland, reduce it further and add more salt to taste. Strain through a fine-mesh strainer into another pot, discard the solids, and let the broth cool before refrigerating or freezing. Store in a tightly sealed container in the refrigerator for at least 5 days and up to 6 months in the freezer.

SEAFOOD BROTH
(Caldo de Mariscos)

This is a "master" seafood stock to use in any seafood recipe, but it's also delicious on its own as a healthy snack, at the beginning of a meal, or as a quick light dish with some fresh shrimp and cooked rice, served with salsa and lime wedges to add to taste.

The best seafood broth is made from a mix of shellfish shells, like shrimp and crab, with parts of the cleaned fish, such as the head, tail, and bones. Most fishmongers, or even the person who works at the fish counter of your local supermarket, can provide you with the best ingredients for seafood broth, but in a pinch you can buy whole fish, ask to have them filleted, and reserve the fillets for another use. The scraps from white fish, such as snapper, grouper, or cod, are best here; the flavors of oily fish like salmon, tuna, or mackerel are too strong to make an all-purpose stock.

1. In a large stockpot, add the shellfish shells, celery, carrots, onion, garlic, rosemary, thyme, and salt plus 3 quarts water. Bring to a boil over high heat, skimming any foam or scum that rises to the surface. Turn the heat down to medium, partly cover the pot, and cook for 2 hours. Keep the broth bubbling gently around the edges but not boiling vigorously. You want the stock to concentrate, but you don't want the liquid to boil away.

2. Taste the broth. It should have a fresh seafood flavor that's pleasant enough to sip straight. You may want to add a little more water if a lot has evaporated or cook longer to further concentrate the flavors. Strain through a fine-mesh strainer into another pot, discard the solids, and let the stock cool before refrigerating or freezing. Tightly covered, it will keep for at least 3 days in the refrigerator and up to 3 months in the freezer.

MAKES ABOUT 2 QUARTS

1½ pounds shellfish shells, fish bones, tails, and heads (use any ratio of shellfish to fish scraps that you like)

4 celery stalks, preferably with leaves, roughly chopped

2 large carrots, cut into thirds

1 medium white onion, quartered

1 head garlic, halved crosswise to expose the cloves

1 fresh rosemary sprig

1 fresh thyme sprig

2 teaspoons kosher salt

TOTAL COOK TIME

3 hours

CHICKEN BROTH
(Caldo de Pollo)

Many chicken broth recipes recommend that you first roast your chicken bones and parts, but we prefer the fresher flavor of boiled chicken. This way the other ingredients—the chiles, vegetables, herbs, and spices—don't get overwhelmed by a heavy roast-chicken flavor. As a bonus, you end up with lots of shredded chicken meat for the fridge or freezer. Even though much of its flavor and moisture will be in the broth, the chicken will still be tasty when mixed with any of our salsas for quick tacos or tostadas, or to add back to this broth for a quick chicken soup.

1. In a large stockpot, add the chicken, onion, garlic, salt, and 3 quarts water. Bring to a boil over high heat and cook, partly covered, for 30 minutes, skimming off any foam or scum that rises to the surface.

2. Add the celery, carrot, parsley, rosemary, and thyme. Turn the heat down to medium and cook for at least 2 hours longer. Keep it at a low simmer so it doesn't evaporate too much.

3. Taste the broth, and, if needed, reduce further to concentrate the flavors. Strain through a fine-mesh strainer into another pot. Pull the chicken meat off the skin and bones and reserve for another use, then discard the other solids. Let the broth cool before refrigerating or freezing. Tightly covered, it will keep at least 3 days in the refrigerator and up to 3 months in the freezer.

MAKES ABOUT 2 QUARTS

3 pounds bone-in chicken parts (preferably legs and wings)

1 medium white onion, quartered

1 head garlic, halved crosswise to expose the cloves

2 teaspoons kosher salt

1 celery stalk, chopped

1 medium carrot, chopped

1 handful fresh parsley sprigs

1 fresh rosemary sprig

1 fresh thyme sprig

TOTAL COOK TIME

3 hours

2
SALSAS THAT MAKE THE MEAL

"Sin salsa no hay comida."

(WITHOUT SALSA, THERE'S NO MEAL.)

—Mama Reyna

Maybe because it rhymes, "sin maíz no hay país" (without corn, there's no country) is a more common refrain in Mexican culinary circles, but we agree with our mother's version. It's just not a proper meal without salsa.

Most of a chile's heat is in its seeds and veins, so, in most cases, we encourage you to remove them before using. You'll still get some chile heat, but it's always easier to add heat than to temper a salsa that's too hot for you to handle. You can seed and devein with your hands (be careful to use gloves or wash your hands thoroughly afterward): Tear off the chile stem, make a lengthwise slit to expose the seeds (so the chile stays intact), and pull out the seeds and veins. You don't have to be very thorough—it's OK to leave behind a few seeds. If your chiles are old and brittle, heating them for about 30 seconds in a hot skillet should make them pliable enough to tear or cut open with a knife. In some cases, dried chiles will have dust or dirt, so just wipe them down before using them.

THE FIRST THING WE NOTICED about Mexican food in the US was the lack of spiciness. We come from a region where chiles are abundant. Breakfast, lunch, dinner, and snacks always have some kind of heat. In the US, though, we found that salsa had notes of sugar and sometimes the consistency reminded us of gravy. We were definitely not used to this. True Mexican salsas are concentrated powerhouses of flavor where a little goes a long way to transform a dish. In most cases, chiles, whether fresh or dried, should be the dominant flavor. Even tomato- or tomatillo-based salsas rely on chiles to make them come alive. Along with onions, chiles add acidity and pungency as well as heat.

It's true that sometimes salsa is often only a condiment served on the side and added in small quantities, but a meal—and, sometimes, an entire restaurant—can rise or fall on the quality of its salsas alone.

Everyone asks for our salsa recipes, so the recipes in this chapter include some of the staples that are synonymous with our food trucks and restaurants, plus many more, from old family favorites to new inventions. Making these salsas will introduce you to ingredients and techniques that you'll find throughout the book.

Since salsas make the meal, as our mother says, in the recipes that follow we make salsa the star and pair it with a super-simple recipe that is basically a foil for the salsa. (For context, one of our favorite "instant" meals involves tearing apart a rotisserie chicken and smothering it with Creamy Jalapeño Salsa [page 73].)

Once you've made these salsas a couple times and earmarked some favorites, you'll have countless low-effort meals at your fingertips. The salsas can be made ahead of time and refrigerated; just bring to room temperature before serving.

Fresh Chiles

HABANERO

One of our favorite chiles, habaneros rank among the world's hottest chiles. They also have a terrific fruity flavor. Scotch bonnet chiles are a cultivar within the same species as habaneros; they're a little sweeter, but can be substituted if necessary. Our "Drunken" Salsa (page 66) and Blackened Habanero Salsa (page 86) make good use of habaneros' flavor as well as their heat.

JALAPEÑO

Jalapeños are named for the city of Jalapa/Xalapa in Veracruz. They're probably our most-used green chile, though serranos are a close second. Try jalapeños in place of serranos in Raw Green Salsa (page 95) or Cooked Tomato Salsa (page 89) to get a sense of their subtle flavor differences.

POBLANO

Mild and deep, poblanos are at their best when roasted over an open flame—the smell of roasting poblano chiles is one of the great Mexican kitchen aromas. We use them in Egg-Tortilla Scramble with Poblano Chiles (page 106), Vegetarian Pozole (page 133), Spaghetti with Poblano Chile Sauce (page 157), and Creamy Poblano Chicken (page 214), but they're a great addition to any vegetarian taco, especially with a little cream and cheese.

SERRANO

Serranos are similar to jalapeños but usually much spicier (spice levels of all fresh chiles can vary widely) and with less of the jalapeño's grassy, bell-pepper flavors. Both jalapeños and serranos are almost always sold green, which is actually their underripe—but no less flavorful—form. We use them in our Cooked Tomato Salsa (page 89) and Cooked Tomatillo Salsa (page 92).

Dried Chiles

ANCHO

Anchos are sweet and almost prune-like, and bring a depth to sauces. They are a key ingredient in Chicken in Red Pumpkin-Seed Sauce (page 217) and Black Mole from Mama's Kitchen (page 210).

CHILE DE ÁRBOL

Chiles de árbol will look familiar to anyone who has used dried chiles in Asian cooking. Varieties like Thai, tianjin, bird's eye, and Indian red chiles are all closely related to chiles de árbol and can be used as substitutes in a pinch. They're hot but with a toasty and vaguely nutty flavor, which takes center stage in Chile de Árbol Salsa (page 74).

CHIPOTLE

Chipotle chiles add smoky flavor to almost any dish. Chiles labeled chipotle, mora, and morita are all dried and smoked jalapeños, just from jalapeño varieties of different sizes. They can be used more or less interchangeably, though we prefer morita for its flavor and familiarity—it's what we used in Veracruz. Canned chipotles are convenient, but due to the sweet sauce they're packed in, they add more sweetness than dried chiles. Chipotles, whether dried or canned, are indispensable in our Garlic-Chipotle Shrimp (page 175), Meatballs in Chipotle Broth (page 194), and Chipotle-Stewed Chicken (page 225).

GUAJILLO

Mild and bright, guajillos are a nice complement to the sweetness of anchos in sauces, like in our Salsa Macha (page 81) and Vegetarian Pozole (page 133). Their brightness is highlighted in Cauliflower "al Pastor" (page 149).

PASILLA

Rich and earthy and delicious in deep dark sauces like mole negro, pasilla chiles add depth to Chile-Roasted Pork (page 202) and Black Mole from Mama's Kitchen (page 210).

PIQUÍN

Chile piquín, often labeled as chiltepín, is tiny and hot (in Veracruz, they're often called chilpaya). When ground, they're a good way to add heat; they are like a more flavorful cayenne powder. We use them in Shrimp in Spicy Cream Sauce (page 188).

"DRUNKEN" SALSA
(Salsa Borracha)

Salsa borracha is traditionally served with slow-cooked meat, known as barbacoa, but it's just as good with "meaty" vegetables like mushrooms, cauliflower, and sweet potatoes. In much of central Mexico, salsa borracha is made with pasilla chiles and pulque (fermented agave sap). Ours is influenced by the North, where it's made with beer (the rest of the bottle is the chef's treat), and by Yucatán, where the fruity but blazing-hot habanero is king. Though you won't get inebriated from a serving of this salsa, nonalcoholic beer works just fine here.

1. In a large bowl, toss the tomatillos, tomatoes, garlic, onion, and habaneros with the oil to coat evenly. Set a heavy skillet (such as cast iron) or a comal set over high heat and cook, turning often, until blackened all over and soft, but not yet turning to ash. Transfer each vegetable to a plate as they finish charring.

2. In a blender, combine the vegetables and the beer and salt. Pulse until almost smooth, then taste and add a little more beer and/or salt, if desired. Serve immediately, or store in a tighly sealed container in the refrigerator for up to 3 days. The salsa will thicken when cold, but can be loosened with a little water.

MAKES ABOUT 1½ CUPS

3 large tomatillos, husked and rinsed (see Note)

2 Roma tomatoes

1 garlic clove, peeled

½ small white onion, halved

2 habanero chiles, stemmed and seeded

2 tablespoons extra-virgin olive oil

2 tablespoons beer (a craft lager or amber ale is best here)

1 teaspoon kosher salt

TOTAL COOK TIME

20 minutes

NOTE

Tomatillos have papery husks and a slightly sticky surface. Simply pull away the husks and rinse them before using.

MUSHROOM QUESADILLAS WITH SALSA BORRACHA

This is our simplified and vegetarian take on barbacoa, the long-cooked meat that is typically served with salsa borracha. If you can't find oyster mushrooms, fresh shiitake or porcini mushrooms have a similarly meaty texture. Here, the salsa's charred notes are great with the chipotles' sweet and smoky flavor.

1. In a large skillet, heat the oil over medium-high heat. Add the garlic and stir for about 30 seconds, then add the mushrooms and chipotles. Fry for about 5 minutes, leaving them mostly untouched, until the mushrooms are tender and a little crispy at the edges. Salt to taste and remove from the heat.

2. Heat a large griddle, comal, or two large skillets over medium heat. Add the tortillas in a single layer and make quesadillas by adding a little mushroom mixture and cheese to half of each tortilla and folding them over (the heat will make the tortillas pliable). Cook, flipping once or twice, until the cheese is melted and the mushrooms are heated through, about 2 minutes. Serve immediately, topped with salsa borracha to taste.

SERVES 4

3 tablespoons extra-virgin olive oil

8 garlic cloves, minced

1 pound oyster mushrooms, torn into thin shreds

3 canned chipotle chiles in adobo, minced to a paste

Kosher salt

12 Corn Tortillas (page 39) or store-bought

8 ounces queso Oaxaca or mozzarella cheese, grated

"Drunken" Salsa (page 66), for serving

TOTAL COOK TIME

25 minutes

TATEMADO:
THE MEXICAN CHAR

Tatemar is a Mexican verb that means to char or toast. It is derived from the Nahuatl *tlatemati*, which is a pre-Columbian cooking method of dry-roasting food (usually vegetables) until deeply charred, and the sugars caramelize. The result is a unique, smoky flavor. With a few exceptions—tortillas, plantains, breaded items, and baked goods—we don't "cook until golden brown," but until our food is as dark as possible. Color equals flavor, and when we want color on vegetables, the darker the better. It's an especially common technique used with tomatoes, tomatillos, garlic, onion, and fresh chiles.

This technique can be achieved by using a cast-iron (or other heavy) pan or griddle—what we call a comal in Mexico. If you have a gas stove, you can place a perforated stainless-steel vegetable steamer basket directly on a gas burner (the heavier the better, and they're not expensive). This lets flames lick the food directly for better flavor, while stopping round ingredients like tomatoes and tomatillos from rolling around when you're trying to char them on all sides. If using a comal or other solid pan, you can lay a sheet of aluminum foil on the bottom so that the vegetables' moisture doesn't stick to the pan, making it harder to clean.

You can call the results charred or even burned, but the goal is to blacken the ingredients on all sides without them turning to ash or giving off too much acrid smoke. Don't let fear cause you to stop charring when it's merely speckled with a few black spots; a longer cook time results in a smokier flavor while making the ingredient even more sweet and tender on the inside.

If for any reason you can't do this on your stovetop, you can also "tatemar" everything on an outdoor grill, under a broiler in a very hot oven, or even in your air fryer on the hottest setting, with the food placed in a single layer without touching.

CREAMY JALAPEÑO SALSA
(Salsa Cremosa de Jalapeño)

MAKES ABOUT 2 CUPS

1½ cups vegetable oil

5 large jalapeño chiles, stemmed

1 small white onion, quartered

1 teaspoon kosher salt

TOTAL COOK TIME

25 minutes

This salsa comes together in a magical way: The hot oil creates an emulsification that results in a creamy sauce without dairy or avocado; the process is similar to that for making mayonnaise, but with hot, not cold fat. This is a decadent salsa, and a little goes a long way. Jalapeño sizes can vary a lot, so if you can't find large ones (at least 4 inches long), just use more.

In a small saucepan, heat the oil over medium heat until it reaches between 175°F and 200°F (a thermometer is ideal here, but if you don't have one, heat until the oil starts to ripple or shimmer slightly without smoking). Add the jalapeños and onion and cook for 10 minutes, then use tongs or a slotted spoon to transfer the jalapeños and onion to a blender. Add the salt and blend until smooth, and then slowly add the hot oil in a thin stream until the mixture comes together as a uniform, emulsified sauce. Taste and add more salt, if needed. Serve immediately, or store in a tightly sealed container in the refrigerator for up to 1 week.

CHICKEN TACOS WITH CREAMY JALAPEÑO SALSA

The richness of this salsa really elevates simple rotisserie chicken and is complemented by the bright onion, cilantro, and lime. Add a crisp salad and it's the perfect weeknight meal.

Tear the chicken meat from its bones, rip the skin into small pieces, and pile on a platter. Serve family-style with hot tortillas, onion, cilantro, salsa, and lime wedges for each guest to make their own tacos.

SERVES 4

1 whole roast chicken, homemade or store-bought, warm or at room temperature

12 corn tortillas (page 39) or store-bought, heated

1 medium white onion, minced

1 bunch cilantro leaves and stems, minced

Creamy Jalapeño Salsa (recipe above), at room temperature, for serving

Lime wedges, for serving

TOTAL COOK TIME

15 minutes

CHILE DE ÁRBOL SALSA
(Salsa de Chile de Árbol)

MAKES ABOUT 2 CUPS

4 Roma tomatoes

¼ cup vegetable oil

30 chiles de árbol, stemmed and seeded

6 garlic cloves, peeled

1 teaspoon kosher salt

TOTAL COOK TIME

45 minutes

A few years after we arrived in the US, my mom ran a tiny kitchen, selling tacos and other antojitos (Mexican street-style snacks) next to a bar on Webberville Road in Austin. Little did we know that years later, we'd buy our first permanent home for Veracruz All Natural just a hundred yards from there. This salsa was a favorite at the shop, especially among her Mexican customers. When we introduced it at Veracruz All Natural, we worried that people would be put off by its spice level, but it's become one of our best-selling salsas and has inspired versions all over Austin. This salsa pairs well with a breakfast taco, since its heat helps wake up the taste buds for the day.

1. In a small saucepan, add the tomatoes and enough water to cover them by an inch. Bring the water to a boil over high heat and cook for 15 minutes, then drain and transfer the tomatoes to a blender.

2. While the tomatoes cook, in a small skillet, heat the oil over medium heat. Add the chiles de árbol and cook, stirring often, until they start to change color but aren't yet burned (when you start seeing or smelling wisps of smoke, take the pan off the heat). Transfer the chiles and oil to the blender with the tomatoes and add the garlic and salt. Blend until smooth. Taste and add salt, if needed. Serve immediately, or store in a tightly sealed container in the refrigerator for up to 5 days.

REFRIED BEANS WITH CHEESE AND CHILE DE ÁRBOL SALSA

Whether as a taco filling or a dip for chips, this dish is a crowd-pleaser any time of day—even on its own as a fiber and protein-packed breakfast with or without eggs.

In a large nonstick skillet, add the beans and and cook over medium heat until very hot throughout. Top with the cheese, turn the heat down to low, cover the pan, and cook just until the cheese melts. Slide the beans onto a plate and top with the onion, cilantro, and salsa to taste. Serve with chips or hot tortillas.

SERVES 4

2 cups Refried Beans (page 49)

4 ounces queso Oaxaca or mozzarella cheese, grated

½ small white onion, minced

½ cup chopped fresh cilantro leaves

Chile de Árbol Salsa (recipe above), for serving

8 ounces unsalted tortilla chips or 12 Corn Tortillas (page 39) or store-bought, heated

TOTAL COOK TIME

10 minutes

SPICY CITRUS SALSA
(Salsa de Cítricos y Piquín)

This inviting salsa was inspired by the piquín chiles in Reyna's garden. We envisioned using them for something bright and fresh to go with Fried Chicken (page 221). Firm believers in balancing flavors in the kitchen, we want almost everything to have something acidic, sweet, and salty—and some chile heat is always a good idea. This salsa is very well balanced. Pair it with any fried food or with raw seafood like tuna sashimi, oysters on the half shell, or scallops (see below).

1. In a small skillet, heat the oil over medium-high heat. Add the piquíns and cook, stirring often, until they start to char, about 1 minute. Transfer to a molcajete (see page 33) or small food processor, add the garlic and salt and grind to a paste.

2. Transfer to a medium-sized bowl and stir in the lime juice, orange juice, cucumber, onion, cilantro, and honey. Mix well and serve immediately, or store in a tightly sealed container in the refrigerator for up to 2 days.

MAKES ABOUT 1½ CUPS

1 tablespoon extra-virgin olive oil

2 teaspoons piquín chiles (see page 65)

4 garlic cloves, peeled

1 teaspoon kosher salt

¼ cup freshly squeezed lime juice

¼ cup freshly squeezed orange juice

¼ cup finely diced cucumber

¼ cup minced red onion

¼ cup minced fresh cilantro leaves

1 teaspoon honey

TOTAL COOK TIME

20 minutes

SCALLOP CRUDO WITH SPICY CITRUS SALSA

SERVES 4

1 pound best-quality sea scallops

Spicy Citrus Salsa (recipe above), for serving

TOTAL PREPARATION TIME

10 minutes

This elegant appetizer—a play on aguachile—comes together in minutes once you've made the salsa. Make it even fancier by serving the scallops on the half shell, if you can find them.

Rinse the scallops and pat them dry. If any have the side muscle (a small tough nub) attached, cut it away and discard. Slice the scallops across the middle into two thin discs. Lay them attractively on a platter and drizzle lightly with the salsa; you will need only a few tablespoons, since you don't want to obscure the scallops' own delicate flavor.

HIBISCUS SALSA
(Salsa de Jamaica)

Best known as a tart and refreshing ingredient in agua fresca, the citrus flavor of flor de Jamaica (dried hibiscus flowers) works well in savory recipes, too (it's usually just called Jamaica, named for the country, and pronounced ha-mai-ka). Flor de Jamaica is easy to find in any Mexican grocery or online. Here, its singular flavor paired with a variety of chiles makes for an especially complex table salsa. Try it with simply grilled meats.

1. In a medium saucepan, add ½ cup of the Jamaica and 1½ cups water and bring to a boil over high heat. Cook for 10 minutes. Strain the liquid into a bowl and set aside. Discard the Jamaica.

2. In a large skillet, heat the oil over medium heat. Working with each type of chile in separate batches, fry them until they become aromatic but before they burn, less than a minute each. As each batch cooks, transfer to a plate, leaving the oil in the pan. Add the garlic to the pan and cook until golden brown. Transfer to the plate with the chiles. Add the remaining 2 cups Jamaica to the pan and cook, stirring just until they heat through, 45 to 60 seconds.

3. In a blender, combine the chiles, garlic, and Jamaica with 1 cup of the reserved Jamaica liquid and puree until very smooth; add more liquid, if needed, to keep the blades turning. This might take 2 minutes or more, since the chiles and Jamaica take a while to break down. If the sauce seems too thick, add a little more Jamaica liquid until it reaches the consistency you desire. Season with the salt. Serve immediately, or store in a tightly sealed container in the refrigerator for up to 3 days.

MAKES ABOUT 2 CUPS

2½ cups flor de Jamaica (dried hibiscus flowers), divided

2 tablespoons extra-virgin olive oil

6 morita chiles (sometimes labeled dried chipotles), stemmed and seeded

2 guajillo chiles, stemmed and seeded

5 chiles de árbol, stemmed and seeded

4 garlic cloves, peeled

2 teaspoons kosher salt

TOTAL COOK TIME
45 minutes

PORK CHOPS WITH HIBISCUS SALSA

Your guests will be shocked at the complexity of this dish if they see how quickly you put it together. If you cook meat more than once a year, we strongly recommend buying a meat thermometer; you can easily find them for less than $10.

1. To dry-brine the pork chops, sprinkle evenly with the salt and place them in a single layer on a wire rack set over a rimmed baking sheet. Refrigerate, uncovered, for at least 4 hours or up to 24 hours.

2. Heat a large cast-iron skillet or grill pan over medium-high heat. Brush off any excess salt from the pork chops with your fingers. Drizzle the oil into the pan and, when hot, add the pork chops in a single layer. Cook until the internal temperature reaches 140°F, about 3 minutes per side, depending on the thickness. Transfer to a plate, cover loosely with aluminum foil, and let rest for 10 minutes.

3. While the pork chops are resting, heat the salsa over low heat. Serve the pork chops on top of the warm salsa.

SERVES 4

4 bone-in pork chops, at least 1 inch thick

2 tablespoons kosher salt

2 tablespoons extra-virgin olive oil

Hibiscus Salsa (page 78), for serving

TOTAL COOK TIME

20 minutes, plus 4 hours brining time

SALSA MACHA

Salsa macha is unique among salsas, with its base of chile-infused oil. It's become more common in the US, but we've long been familiar with it from Veracruz, where it's usually made with a very spicy but flavorful chile called comapeño. Don't be deterred by the five different chiles used here. They're key to the salsa's complexity, and it's just as easy to buy small amounts of five chiles as it is to buy a big bag of one type. This recipe is a good way to familiarize yourself with the textures and aromas of each chile. When stemming and seeding, don't worry if some seeds are left behind.

1. In a small saucepan, heat the oil over medium heat. Add the onion and garlic and cook for 12 to 15 minutes, until the onion and garlic turn golden brown; if they seem to be "deep-frying" or cooking too fast, reduce the heat a little.

2. With a slotted spoon, transfer the onion and garlic to a blender. Add one-third of the chiles to the hot oil and fry them only until they start to change color and smell a little toasty, less than 30 seconds. Repeat this step two more times. Be careful not to burn them, or the salsa will taste bitter. Reserve the oil in the pan.

3. Add the chiles to the blender, along with the sesame seeds and the salt. With the blender running, slowly add all the oil in a thin stream. The salsa should have a uniform consistency but still retain some texture. Taste and add more salt to taste.

4. Serve right away, or store in a tightly sealed container in the refrigerator for up to 1 month.

MAKES ABOUT 2 CUPS

2 cups extra-virgin olive oil

1 small white onion, quartered

15 garlic cloves, peeled

15 guajillo chiles, stemmed and seeded

5 ancho chiles, stemmed and seeded

10 morita chiles, stemmed and seeded

10 chiles de árbol, stemmed and seeded

2 tablespoons piquín chiles

¼ cup toasted sesame seeds

2 teaspoons kosher salt

TOTAL COOK TIME
45 minutes

SALMON WITH SALSA MACHA

Salsa macha is an amazing addition to fatty meats and oily fish like salmon, tuna, and trout. This parchment-baking method keeps the salmon moist—it essentially steams it—but you can bake, grill, roast, or use any cooking method you like. Since the only added flavoring here is the salsa, use the best-quality fish you can find.

1. Heat the oven to 400°F. Coat the salmon fillets evenly with the salt and place each one on a piece of parchment paper large enough to enclose the fillets. Fold the parchment over the salmon so that no liquid can leak out and the packet can't unfold in the oven. Place the parchment packets on a rimmed baking sheet and bake for about 15 minutes, or until the center of the fish is opaque and flakes easily with a fork.

2. Serve each fillet on an individual plate for each guest to open the packet themselves, later adding the salsa to taste.

SERVES 4

4 (6- to 8-ounce) salmon fillets

1 teaspoon kosher salt

Salsa Macha (page 81), for serving

TOTAL COOK TIME

20 minutes

SPICY GREEN SALSA
(Salsa Macha Verde)

This salsa is for people who love lime. The lime here cuts through the heat, giving the salsa a perfect balance of spiciness and acidity. By quick-frying the jalapeño and onion, this salsa develops a deep charred flavor while still retaining the fresh vibrancy of a salsa cruda (uncooked salsa).

Try this salsa with anything fried, such as Bean Gorditas (page 52), Potato Taquitos (page 161), or Pan-Fried Cauliflower Steaks (page 162). Because we had the right ingredients on hand, a version of this salsa was always on our table growing up.

In a small cast-iron skillet, heat the oil over high heat. Add the jalapeños and onion and cook until the vegetables are evenly charred on all sides—they should almost blacken on the outside but not cook all the way through. Transfer the jalapeños and onion to a blender, along with the garlic, avocado, lime juice, and salt. Blend until smooth. This salsa is best served the day it is made.

MAKES ABOUT 1 CUP

1 teaspoon extra-virgin olive oil

4 large jalapeños, stemmed

½ small white onion

2 garlic cloves, peeled

½ avocado, diced

¼ cup freshly squeezed lime juice

¼ teaspoon kosher salt

TOTAL COOK TIME

15 minutes

SPICY CHICKEN WINGS

SERVES 4

5 pounds chicken wings, separated into drums and flats

2 tablespoons baking powder

1 tablespoon kosher salt

Spicy Green Salsa (recipe above), for serving

TOTAL COOK TIME

1 hour

Think of this as a Mexican take on Buffalo wings. Baking the wings makes them a little healthier, though no less satisfying, than frying. The baking powder keeps them crispy as they fry.

1. Heat the oven to 450°F. Place a wire rack over a rimmed baking sheet.

2. Pat the chicken dry with paper towels. In a large mixing bowl, toss the chicken with the baking powder and salt. Transfer to the wire rack in a single layer. Bake for 45 minutes, flipping the wings after 25 minutes. At the end of the cooking time, cut into a big one to make sure they're cooked through.

3. To serve, you can toss the wings with salsa to taste for a "finger licking" presentation, drizzle with salsa, or serve with salsa on the side. An accompanying cold beer or a good mezcal can't hurt, either.

BLACKENED HABANERO SALSA
(Salsa Negra)

This recipe is inspired by the Yucatán, where the blazingly spicy habanero chile is king, and a version of this salsa can be found on most tables. Cooking chiles, whether charring or boiling, tempers their heat. The tortillas and husks are indeed burned here, but somehow, once everything is blended together with oil, this sauce doesn't taste burned or bitter, just deep and earthy. It pairs well with any simple corn-based dish like Picadas (page 42) or Empanadas (page 43). The corn husks lend a wonderfully earthy flavor, but they can be left out, if desired.

1. Using a comal, wire rack, or steel steamer basket (see Tatemado, page 70) set over a high-heat gas flame, cook the habaneros, garlic, and onion until everything is blackened all over but not yet turning to ash. The smaller vegetables will tend to finish before the large vegetables. As each piece blackens—you want them completely charred all over—transfer to a plate with tongs.

2. Add the tortillas and cook until burned, then transfer to the plate with tongs. Finally, add the corn husks and cook until burned (be careful, as they will crumble once burned), and transfer to the plate. When working over an open flame, move the tortillas and corn husks often so they don't catch fire, and simply blow out any flames if they do. Remove the peels from the garlic and discard.

3. In a blender, add everything, along with the salt and oil, and blend until smooth. Serve immediately, or store in a tightly sealed container in the refrigerator for up to 5 days.

MAKES ABOUT 1½ CUPS

12 habanero chiles (preferably green), stemmed and seeded

8 large garlic cloves, unpeeled

1 medium white onion, cut into 8 pieces

2 Corn Tortillas (page 39) or store-bought

2 corn husks (just the husks, from 2 ears fresh corn)

1 teaspoon kosher salt

¾ cup extra-virgin olive oil

TOTAL COOK TIME
20 minutes

STEAK TACOS WITH SALSA NEGRA

Pounding beef before cooking it not only tenderizes it, but also allows it to cook very quickly. If you already have the salsa on hand, this satisfying dinner can be made in fifteen minutes.

1. Season the meat all over with salt and pepper. Set aside.

2. Trim the scallions by cutting off the root ends and the tips of the green tops. Slice them in half lengthwise. In a medium bowl, toss with the oil and salt and pepper to taste. Heat a large, heavy skillet (preferably cast iron) or griddle over high heat and add the scallions, stirring occasionally until they are charred and tender, about 5 minutes. Transfer to a plate.

3. Add the meat in batches to the pan and cook for about 1 minute on each side, or until cooked to your desired doneness.

4. Slice the steak across the grain and divide it equally among the tortillas. Top with scallions and cilantro. Have guests squeeze lime over the tacos and add salsa to taste.

SERVES 4 TO 6

2 pounds skirt steak or flank steak, cut into several pieces and pounded to ¼-inch thickness

Kosher salt and freshly ground black pepper

2 bunches scallions (about 16)

1 tablespoon extra-virgin olive oil

12 Corn Tortillas (page 39) or store-bought, or flour tortillas, warmed

¾ cup minced fresh cilantro leaves

4 limes, quartered

Blackened Habanero Salsa (page 86), for serving

TOTAL COOK TIME

25 minutes

COOKED TOMATO SALSA
(Salsa Ranchera)

It doesn't get more simple than this salsa, which can be served with almost anything. It was probably the most-requested salsa at our mom's fonda in Veracruz because it suits everyone's palate, and it's equally popular at our restaurant Veracruz Fonda & Bar. Though we prefer to make it with serranos, you can substitute jalapeños if that's what you have on hand. The hot tomatoes will soften the garlic as it blends, so you'll get a combination of the raw garlic's punch and the cooked garlic's sweetness. In Veracruz, you often see this salsa with onion added (boiled with the tomatoes and chiles) and minced cilantro stirred in at the end. Feel free to experiment.

MAKES ABOUT 4 CUPS

12 Roma tomatoes

6 serrano chiles, stemmed

10 garlic cloves, peeled

1½ teaspoons kosher salt

2 tablespoons vegetable oil

TOTAL COOK TIME

30 minutes

1. In a small saucepan, combine the tomatoes and serranos and pour in enough water to cover the vegetables by 1 inch. Bring to a boil over high heat and cook for 15 minutes, then drain. In a blender, combine the tomatoes and chiles along with the garlic and salt. Blend until smooth.

2. Heat the oil in the same saucepan over medium heat. When it starts to shimmer, turn the heat down to low and add the salsa (careful, it will splatter, so stir constantly). Cook for 1 minute, or until it thickens to your desired consistency. Serve immediately, or store in a tightly sealed container in the refrigerator for up to 3 days.

HUEVOS RANCHEROS

You can, of course, prepare the eggs however you like for this dish—fried, poached, boiled—but scrambled makes this recipe super easy and exceptionally convenient for a group meal. Refried Beans (page 49) are terrific on the side.

1. In a large skillet, heat the oil over medium-high heat. When the edge of a tortilla sizzles on contact, fry the tortillas in batches until they are firm but still a little pliable, about 20 seconds per side. Drain them on a paper towel–lined plate.

2. When all the tortillas are fried, add the eggs to the same pan and scramble over low heat until they're set but still moist, 1 to 2 minutes. To assemble the huevos rancheros, lightly coat four plates with salsa, overlap two tortillas on each plate, and top with the eggs and more salsa. Serve with the avocado, queso fresco, and cilantro.

SERVES 4

$\frac{1}{4}$ cup vegetable oil

8 Corn Tortillas (page 39) or store-bought

8 large eggs, beaten

Cooked Tomato Salsa (page 89), for serving

1 avocado, pitted, peeled, and sliced, for serving

$\frac{1}{2}$ cup crumbled queso fresco, for serving

$\frac{1}{4}$ packed cup fresh cilantro leaves, minced, for serving

TOTAL COOK TIME

15 minutes

COOKED TOMATILLO SALSA
(Salsa Tomatillo)

This salsa is a must for Green Chilaquiles (page 109), but it's also a good everyday salsa. The popular Mexican dish called verdolagas en salsa verde uses a version of this salsa as the base for stewing greens with chicken or pork.

Because of tomatillos' high pectin content, tomatillo salsas thicken when refrigerated. It will thin as it comes to room temperature or when cooked, but if you're using this salsa straight from the fridge, we recommend stirring in a little water.

MAKES ABOUT 4 CUPS

15 large tomatillos (about 2 pounds), husked and rinsed

6 serrano chiles, stemmed

8 garlic cloves, peeled

¾ packed cup fresh cilantro leaves

1 tablespoon kosher salt

3 tablespoons vegetable oil

TOTAL COOK TIME

30 minutes

1. In a medium saucepan, combine the tomatillos and serranos and pour in enough water to cover them by 1 inch. Bring to a boil over high heat and cook for 15 minutes, then drain. Transfer the tomatillos and chiles to a blender, along with the garlic, cilantro, and salt. Blend until very smooth.

2. In the same saucepan, heat the oil over high heat. When it starts to shimmer, turn the heat down to low and add the salsa (careful, it will splatter, so stir constantly). Cook, stirring often, for about 1 minute, or until it thickens to your desired consistency. Serve immediately, or store in a tightly sealed container in the refrigerator for up to 3 days.

BREAKFAST PICADAS

SERVES 2

2 Picadas (page 42)

Cooked Tomatillo Salsa (recipe above), for serving

¼ cup crumbled queso fresco

2 tablespoons minced white onion

4 large eggs

½ avocado, peeled and cut into 4 slices

TOTAL COOK TIME

15 minutes

We could eat these every day—and not just for breakfast. Like tacos, you can top these with any salsa and any meat or vegetable, but this combination of tomatillo salsa with egg on top is a favorite at any time of day.

1. Heat the picadas on the griddle or comal used to cook them. As they heat, top with salsa, queso fresco, and onion, in that order (this both looks most appealing, and lets the salsa heat through). In the meantime, fry the eggs in a separate pan to your desired doneness.

2. To serve, place the picadas on plates, top each with two fried eggs and two avocado slices. Serve with additional salsa to taste.

RAW GREEN SALSA
(Salsa Verde Cruda)

Most raw salsa verde recipes are similar—a puree of tomatillos, cilantro, onion, and chiles. We find that a small amount of olive oil and honey (and avocado) is transformative. The oil provides richness and the honey balances some of the tomatillos' sour notes. There's barely any ingredient prep for this salsa, which comes together almost instantly. On a hectic weekday evening, this salsa brings to life any combination of leftover meat, veggies, rice, and beans with hot fresh or store-bought tortillas. We prefer to use serranos here, but you can use jalapeños as well.

In a blender, combine the tomatillos, garlic, serranos, cilantro, onion, lime juice, oil, salt, honey, and half of the avocado. Pulse until it's a coarse puree. Taste and add more salt, honey, lime, or chile, as desired. Cut the remaining avocado half into a small dice and stir it into the salsa. Serve immediately; this salsa is best eaten fresh.

MAKES ABOUT 1½ CUPS

6 large tomatillos, husked, rinsed, and halved

4 garlic cloves, peeled

3 serrano chiles, stemmed

¾ packed cup fresh cilantro leaves

¼ small white onion

1 tablespoon freshly squeezed lime juice (about ½ lime)

1 tablespoon extra-virgin olive oil

1 teaspoon kosher salt

1 teaspoon honey

1 large avocado, halved, pitted, and peeled

TOTAL PREPARATION TIME

10 minutes

FRIED PLANTAINS AND RICE WITH SALSA VERDE CRUDA

SERVES 4

¼ cup vegetable oil

2 very ripe plantains, peeled and cut diagonally into ½-inch slices

2 to 3 cups White Rice (page 46), hot

Raw Green Salsa (recipe above), for serving

TOTAL COOK TIME

15 minutes, plus rice cooking time

NOTE

If using leftover rice, reheat it on the stovetop or microwave and keep warm while you fry the plantains.

Adding this tart fresh salsa to sweet plantain turns a simple side dish into a meal. It's also a terrific use for leftover rice. Ripe plantains are mostly black with some yellow spots. They will ripen in a warm kitchen, but you can speed along the ripening by wrapping them in newspaper and baking for thirty minutes in a 300°F oven (don't worry—at this temperature, the newspaper won't catch fire!).

In a large skillet, heat the oil over high heat. Add the plantains in a single layer and cook until they are deeply browned on both sides, 2 to 3 minutes per side. Transfer to a plate. Serve the rice on a platter with the plantains draped in a single layer over the rice. Add salsa to taste.

VEGAN QUESO

We hadn't had Tex-Mex "queso"—a (usually) processed cheese spread—before coming to the US. We love it (who doesn't like queso?), but it was never something we felt comfortable eating on a regular basis. We assigned ourselves the challenge of making a vegan version made from natural, unprocessed ingredients, so that both we and our guests could indulge more often. Over time, with endless trial and error, we developed this version that you can eat guiltlessly by the spoonful.

1. In a heatproof bowl, add the cashews and cover with boiling water. Let soak for 1 hour. Drain well and transfer the cashews to a blender, along with the garlic, nutritional yeast, coconut milk, salt, and lime juice. Blend until very smooth and creamy, adding more water, if needed, to turn the blades.

2. In a large saucepan, heat the oil over medium-high heat. Add the onion and cook until golden brown, about 5 minutes. Turn the heat down to low and add the paste from the blender. Stir in the warm water, jalapeños, and red bell pepper. Cook, stirring often, for about 3 minutes, or until it has the classic silky "queso" texture of melted cheese, somewhere between a sauce and a dip. Serve immediately, or store in a tightly sealed container in the refrigerator for up to 5 days.

MAKES ABOUT 4 CUPS

8 ounces raw unsalted cashews

2 garlic cloves, peeled

2 tablespoons nutritional yeast

1 cup unsweetened coconut milk

1 tablespoon kosher salt

1 tablespoon freshly squeezed lime juice

2 tablespoons extra-virgin olive oil

½ medium white onion, minced

2 cups warm water

8 medium jalapeño chiles, stemmed, seeded, and minced

½ red bell pepper, stemmed, seeded, and minced

TOTAL COOK TIME

30 minutes, plus 1 hour soaking time

LOADED VEGAN NACHOS

SERVES 4

4 ounces unsalted tortilla chips

1 cup Refried Beans (page 49) or store-bought

½ cup canned pickled jalapeños, drained

½ cup diced fresh tomato

½ cup minced white onion

1 avocado, pitted, peeled, and cut into small dice

1 recipe Vegan Queso (recipe above)

TOTAL COOK TIME

20 minutes

These simple nachos let the queso shine, while the beans add extra heft and depth, and vegetables add freshness and contrast.

Heat the oven to 400°F. Arrange the tortilla chips in a single, slightly overlapping layer on a rimmed baking sheet. Distribute the beans, jalapeños, tomato, onion, and avocado over the chips. Add the Vegan Queso to cover everything almost entirely. Bake until the nachos are bubbly and hot throughout, about 10 minutes.

PUMPKIN SEED–TOMATO DIP
(Sikil Pak)

Mayans have made a version of this classic Yucatecan dip (*sikil* means pumpkin seed and *p'aak* means tomato in Yucatecan Maya) for millennia. Dry-frying native ingredients like tomatoes and squash seeds over a fire and grinding them in a molcajete (see page 33) is emblematic of Indigenous Mexican cooking and connects us with our roots. You can make this in a molcajete for maximum flavor, but, admittedly, it does take forever to crush the seeds to a paste until they release their oil; it's like making peanut butter by hand. So we use a blender. This is a terrific appetizer served with tostadas or fried tortilla chips (totopos).

MAKES 2 CUPS

8 ounces raw pepitas (pumpkin seeds)

3 Roma tomatoes

1 small white onion, quartered

3 serrano chiles, stemmed

8 garlic cloves, peeled

1 teaspoon kosher salt

TOTAL COOK TIME

20 minutes

1. In a heavy skillet, add the pumpkin seeds and cook over high heat, stirring constantly, until they are dark and fragrant (most of them will "pop" and puff up) but not burned. Transfer to a blender.

2. Using a comal, wire rack, or steel steamer basket (see Tatemado, page 70) set over a high-heat gas flame, cook the tomatoes, onion, serranos, and garlic until everything is blackened all over but not yet turning to ash. The small vegetables will tend to finish before the large vegetables. As each vegetable blackens, transfer it to the blender.

3. Add the salt to the blender and blend everything until smooth. It will take a couple minutes to break the pumpkin seeds down to a paste. The mixture will thicken a little as it cools. Serve at room temperature. It is best when made the same day but will keep in a tightly sealed container in the refrigerator for up to 5 days.

ROASTED VEGETABLES WITH PUMPKIN SEED–TOMATO DIP

The richness of the Mayan dip sikil pak is particularly good when balanced with vegetables. Try grilling the vegetables over an open fire or roasting them in a 500°F oven for 15 minutes to add a charred element that complements the charred tomato notes in the sauce.

Heat the oven to 450°F. In a large mixing bowl, toss the vegetables with the oil and salt. Spread them in a single layer on a rimmed baking sheet. Bake for about 20 minutes, or until tender and starting to brown at the edges. Serve the vegetables on top of the sikil pak, or dollop the sauce on top.

SERVES 4

1½ pounds mixed firm vegetables (such as broccoli, asparagus, carrots, cauliflower, or zucchini), cut into 1-inch chunks

1 tablespoon extra-virgin olive oil

1½ teaspoons kosher salt

Pumpkin Seed–Tomato Dip (page 97), at room temperature, for serving

TOTAL COOK TIME

30 minutes

3
BREAKFAST ALL NATURAL— AND ALL DAY

"Desayunar como rey, comer como príncipe, y cenar como mendigo."

(EAT BREAKFAST LIKE A KING, LUNCH LIKE A PRINCE, AND DINNER LIKE A PAUPER.)

We've been rule benders all of our lives—even with something as simple as breakfast. Most of our food trucks open at 7:00 a.m., and although the migas and breakfast tacos are most popular, if you want shrimp macha, mole negro, or al pastor tacos at an early hour, we've got you covered.

BREAKFAST, HOWEVER, ISN'T JUST A morning meal for us. Just like steak and fish tacos are as good for breakfast as they are for lunch, we also eat typical breakfast dishes all day long. As kids, we loved "breakfast for dinner" (not realizing it was an economic choice, not meant as a treat!) and we still do. Eggs are a perfect protein any time of day, especially for people looking to eat less— or no—meat.

Our mother was all about being resourceful with our limited income and making the most of what was already in the fridge. Assuming you usually have eggs and corn tortillas, you can create your own version of migas using any leftover meat and vegetables. For us, because of our mother's influence, creating a meal with what's already in the fridge is an opportunity for creativity, not a frustrating challenge. Sometimes the best dishes are born out of necessity.

The fact that our migas taco is often called the best in Austin is both ironic and flattering because it was the taco that confused us the most when we came to Austin. In Spanish, *migas* simply means "crumbs," and there are various regional dishes called migas. In most of central Mexico, it's a garlicky, meaty bread soup. In Sinaloa, it's a spongy corn-based dessert. In Veracruz, we knew migas as a scramble of eggs with leftover fried tortillas, tomato, onion, and chile, served family-style with beans and salsas at any time of day, always paired with some fresh tortillas for you to build your own taco. The version of migas we saw when we arrived in Texas was different—it was a little more soggy, made with thinner store-bought chips, some even drenched in salsa. The tortillas-in-a-tortilla concept of a migas taco seemed even stranger.

Eventually we started thinking about why Austin migas never matched our memories of the migas back home. It's not that the ingredients are so complex, or that it's a difficult recipe. We discovered that it's all in the *quality* of the ingredients. More important, our tortilla chips are all homemade—intact and still a little crunchy—and we make this dish to order so that it's fresh for each of our customers. This combination gives our migas the flavors and textures we missed so much, transporting us back to Veracruz. If you must use store-bought chips, try to find very good-quality, thick, unsalted ones. But promise us to make this just once with homemade chips to taste the difference.

JALAPEÑO-EGG FRITTER
(Torta de Huevo con Venas de Jalapeño)

Our Tía Carmela was one of the oldest of my mom's eleven siblings, and she was usually the one in charge of feeding the entire family. We grew up marveling at her creativity and her ability to stretch out the little food they could afford. We wanted to include this recipe because it showcases her ingenuity. Every time she made chiles rellenos, she'd set aside the jalapeño veins and seeds instead of throwing them away. When we asked why she did this, she said, "This is another meal." It was a lesson in using what most people would consider "scraps" to envision a completely new dish. Since the veins and seeds are the spiciest part (be careful when handling them), you'd expect this dish to be overly spicy, but the other ingredients temper the heat considerably. Tía Carmela always knew exactly what she was doing.

Make this dish with the jalapeño "guts" from Cold Tuna-Stuffed Jalapeño Chiles (page 178), or buy jalapeños specifically for this dish and use the leftover chiles in any of our green salsas, roasted with other vegetables, or scrambled with eggs.

1. In a large bowl, lightly beat the eggs with the garlic powder and ½ teaspoon of the salt; set aside.

2. In a large nonstick pan (one that has a lid), heat the oil over medium heat. Add the jalapeño veins, red bell pepper, mushrooms, onion, garlic, black pepper, and the remaining 1 teaspoon salt, and sauté until the vegetables are tender, about 5 minutes.

3. Turn the heat down to low and wait 1 minute for the temperature of the pan contents to come down so the eggs don't cook too quickly. Add the egg mixture evenly over the vegetables, cover the pan, and cook to your desired level of doneness, usually about 10 minutes (shake the pan to see if some of the egg is still liquid). Transfer to a serving plate and top with queso fresco and salsa. Serve the torta on its own or in tacos topped with beans, avocado, and more salsa, if desired.

SERVES 4

5 large eggs

½ teaspoon garlic powder

1½ teaspoons kosher salt, divided

1 tablespoon extra-virgin olive oil

1 cup jalapeño chile veins (scraped from halved chiles)

½ cup diced red bell pepper

½ cup sliced mushrooms (any type)

½ cup diced white onion

1 garlic clove, minced

¼ teaspoon freshly ground black pepper

Crumbled queso fresco and salsa of your choice, for topping

Corn Tortillas (page 39) or store-bought)

Refried Beans (page 49), chopped avocado, and/or additional salsa, for serving (optional)

TOTAL COOK TIME

30 minutes

EGG-TORTILLA SCRAMBLE
(Migas)

For the best migas, make homemade chips; they really are part of the magic. It adds just a few more minutes to the preparation, and it's worth it. And even though eggs should usually be cooked over low heat, high heat is crucial here so the migas cook quickly enough that the chips don't get soggy.

1. To make the chips, in a small saucepan or deep skillet, heat the oil over medium-high heat. When it's hot enough that the edge of a tortilla sizzles aggressively on contact, add the tortilla pieces, making sure they don't stick together. Working in batches, toss the pieces gently in the oil, ensuring that every part of each tortilla gets some oil on it, for about 2 minutes, or until golden brown and crisp. Remove the pieces with a slotted spoon or tongs and place them on a paper towel–lined plate to drain. Reserve the oil.

2. To make the migas, in a large nonstick skillet, add 3 tablespoons of the hot cooking oil (discard the rest, or strain and reuse) and heat over medium-high heat. Add the onion and stir for 30 seconds, add the garlic and stir for 45 seconds, then add the tomatoes and cilantro and stir for 45 seconds more. Add the eggs and chips, stir gently to combine, then add the salt and pepper. Cook, stirring often but gently so you don't break the chips, for about 2 minutes, or until the eggs are no longer runny but the chips are still firm. Sprinkle the cheese over the top and when it starts to melt, remove the pan from the heat. Add the avocado before serving. Serve on their own or in tacos, if desired, with your choice of salsa at the table.

SERVES 2

FOR THE CHIPS:

1 cup vegetable oil

4 store-bought corn tortillas, preferably stale, each cut into 6 wedges

FOR THE MIGAS:

½ cup diced white onion

4 garlic cloves, minced

1 cup diced Roma tomatoes (about 2 tomatoes), drained

½ cup minced fresh cilantro leaves

8 large eggs, beaten

1 teaspoon kosher salt

1 teaspoon freshly ground black pepper

½ cup grated Monterey Jack cheese

1 avocado, pitted, peeled, and cut into cubes

Corn Tortillas (page 39) or store-bought, for serving (optional)

Raw Green Salsa (page 95), Creamy Jalapeño Salsa (page 73), or Chile de Árbol Salsa (page 74), for serving

TOTAL COOK TIME
45 minutes

EGG-TORTILLA SCRAMBLE WITH POBLANO CHILES
(Migas Poblanas)

1. To make the chips, in a small saucepan or deep skillet, heat the oil over medium-high heat. When it's hot enough that the edge of a tortilla sizzles aggressively on contact, add the tortilla pieces, making sure they don't stick together. Working in batches, toss the pieces gently in the oil, ensuring that every part of each tortilla gets some oil on it, for about 2 minutes, or until golden brown and crisp. Remove the pieces with a slotted spoon or tongs and place them on a paper towel–lined plate to drain. Reserve the oil.

2. To make the migas, roast the poblano chile by placing it directly over a gas flame or under a broiler. Turn it often until the skin is blackened but not disintegrated. Place it in a ziplock bag or covered bowl for at least 5 minutes. When it's cool enough to handle, gently peel the charred skin (it's OK if some remains), then make a lengthwise slit and carefully remove the seeds, veins, and stem. Slice thinly and set aside.

3. In a large nonstick skillet, add 3 tablespoons of the hot cooking oil (discard the rest, or strain and reuse) and heat over medium-high heat. Add the poblano and onion and stir for 30 seconds, then add garlic and stir for another 45 seconds. Add the eggs and chips, stir gently to combine, then add the salt and pepper. Cook, stirring often but gently so you don't break the chips, for 2 minutes, or until the egg is no longer runny but the chips are still firm. Sprinkle the beans and cheese over the top and heat through. Scatter the avocado on top before serving. Serve on their own or in tacos, if desired, adding salsa at the table.

SERVES 2

FOR THE CHIPS:

1 cup vegetable oil

4 store-bought corn tortillas, preferably stale, each cut into 6 wedges

FOR THE MIGAS:

1 poblano chile

½ cup thinly sliced white onion

4 garlic cloves, minced

8 large eggs, beaten

1 teaspoon kosher salt

1 teaspoon freshly ground black pepper

1 cup Refried Beans (page 49) or rinsed and drained canned black beans, warmed

½ cup crumbled queso fresco

1 avocado, pitted, peeled, and cut into cubes

Corn Tortillas (page 39) or store-bought, for serving (optional)

Salsa of your choice, for serving

TOTAL COOK TIME
45 minutes

GREEN CHILAQUILES
(Chilaquiles Verdes)

When we were kids, in order to save oil to fry tortillas for my mom's fonda, we put our tortillas out in the sun to dry so they absorbed less oil when frying. As adults, we appreciate the healthy implications of this, not to mention that dried-out tortillas have better crunch and flavor when fried. These have been hugely popular since the first time we sold them from our original food truck on César Chávez Street. Locals immediately gravitated to the heartiness of the dish—Austinites love their weekend brunch!—as well as the freshly made salsa and its simple authenticity.

1. In a deep skillet, add the oil to a depth of about ¼ inch; you may need more or less oil depending on your pan size. Heat over medium-high heat to between 350°F and 375°F, or until the corner of a tortilla sizzles aggressively on contact.

2. Working in batches, add the tortilla pieces one at a time, so that they're not sitting on top of each other, and fry them for about 2 minutes per side, or until they're golden brown and crisp. It's OK if some aren't perfectly crispy since they will be soaking in sauce later anyway. Remove the pieces with a slotted spoon or tongs and place them on a paper towel–lined plate to drain.

3. When all the tortillas have been fried, save or discard the remaining oil and turn the heat down to medium. Add the salsa and chips, mixing well to ensure they're all well coated with sauce. When the chips start to soften and the sauce thickens a little, remove the pan from the heat and divide the chilaquiles among four plates. To serve, top each with a fried egg, if desired, and garnish with the onion, cheese, and crema.

SERVES 4

1 to 2 cups vegetable oil

16 store-bought corn tortillas, preferably left to dry at room temperature for at least 1 and up to 12 hours, quartered

4 cups Cooked Tomatillo Salsa (page 92)

4 fried eggs (optional)

1 medium white onion, very thinly sliced

1 cup crumbled queso fresco (about 5 ounces)

½ cup Mexican crema

red pepper flakes, for garnish

TOTAL COOK TIME

45 minutes (varies depending on pan size)

TIPS

For chilaquiles rojos, use Cooked Tomato Salsa (page 89) in place of the tomatillo salsa.

Feel free to add seared thin-sliced beef or chicken in place of, or in addition to, the egg.

Chilaquiles are always made better when paired with a spoonful of Refried Beans (page 49) on the side.

EL BREAKFAST TACO

El Breakfast Taco isn't even the right name for this taco because we could eat it all day, every day. This taco sells all day long at our taco trucks. The key to a great breakfast taco—and any great dish, really—is using the very best ingredients you can find.

Two simple things make a big difference here: We cut the bacon finely so that there's some in every bite, and we cook the eggs in the same pan where everything else has cooked so they absorb all that flavor from the other ingredients.

1. In a large skillet, heat the oil over medium heat and add the bacon. Cook, stirring occasionally, until the bacon releases its fat and starts to crisp at the edges, about 5 minutes. With a slotted spoon, transfer the bacon to a paper towel–lined plate, leaving the fat in the pan. Add the potatoes to the pan and cook, stirring occasionally to coat in the fat, until they become golden brown all over, 10 to 15 minutes. Add the onion and stir for about 1 minute, until it softens. Add the garlic and cook, stirring occasionally, until the potatoes are soft throughout, about 3 minutes. Add the serrano and cook for about 30 seconds, then stir in the eggs, salt, and pepper. Stir gently, coating everything in the pan, until the eggs are set to your liking.

2. Divide the egg mixture among the tortillas and top with avocado, cheese, and salsa. Serve.

Everything's a Breakfast Taco

Coming to Austin and finding breakfast tacos everywhere was surprising, but not a foreign concept. In Mexico, we make everything into tacos. Tacos with eggs, nopales, potato and chorizo, barbacoa, and tacos de canasta (steamed tacos sold by street vendors) are all common examples of breakfast tacos to us. In this spirit, shake off the idea that breakfast tacos must include eggs; any taco eaten for breakfast is a breakfast taco.

That said, eggs are about the easiest protein with which to fill tacos. At home, we make breakfast tacos with whatever is left over in our fridges. Luckily, we tend to always have certain basics: eggs, beans, vegetables, and salsas. Follow our lead by first sautéing onion, fresh chile, and garlic in oil, then adding eggs (scrambled with leftover veggies, meat, or other protein, if you want). Serve on top of fresh tortillas and add beans, avocado, queso fresco, and any salsa you like to make a fast, filling, and nutritious breakfast at any time of the day.

SERVES 4

1 tablespoon extra-virgin olive oil

8 strips bacon, finely chopped

1½ pounds Yukon Gold (or other variety) potatoes, peeled and cut into small dice (¼ to ½ inch)

½ small white onion, diced

2 garlic cloves, minced

1 serrano chile, stemmed and minced

8 large eggs, beaten

1½ teaspoons kosher salt

1 teaspoon freshly ground black pepper

8 Corn Tortillas (page 39) or store-bought, warmed

1 avocado, pitted, peeled, and cut into 16 slices

1 cup grated Monterey Jack cheese (about 4 ounces)

Salsa of your choice, for serving

TOTAL COOK TIME

30 minutes

TIPS

Instead of the bacon, you can use 8 ounces fresh Mexican chorizo, removed from the casing. Break it up into little pieces as it cooks.

If using store-bought tortillas that are particularly small, thin, or fragile, use two per taco.

These are especially good with Refried Beans (page 49) on the side.

TORTILLAS IN BEAN SAUCE
(Enfrijoladas)

For us, this dish is pure comfort food and infallible to boot: If your beans are great, your enfrijoladas will be, too. Feel free to make enfrijoladas as simple or as complex as you like by adding fillings or toppings, such as scrambled or fried eggs, cooked meat, or stir-fried veggies. Just don't skip the step of frying the tortillas; it has a huge impact on both flavor and texture.

1. To make the bean sauce, in a large skillet, heat the oil over medium-high heat. Add the onion and garlic and cook, stirring often, until golden brown, about 5 minutes. Add the beans, coconut milk, and salt and cook, stirring often, for another 5 minutes. Transfer to a blender and puree until very smooth. Return the bean sauce to the skillet and keep warm over low heat while you finish the dish.

2. In another medium skillet, heat the oil over medium-high heat. Test the oil by dipping the edge of a tortilla into it; if it sizzles, it's hot enough. Using tongs, dip the tortillas in the oil one at a time for 30 to 45 seconds—long enough for them to be pliable without breaking, but not long enough that they start to get hard (you may want to practice with one or two extra tortillas).

3. As you fry them, shake any excess oil back into the pan, then stack the tortillas on a plate (don't worry about any excess oil that sticks to them). When all the tortillas are fried, dunk them one at a time in the bean sauce to coat evenly, then transfer them to a plate, folding each tortilla in half. Garnish with queso fresco and onion. Serve hot, as the sauce thickens when it cools.

SERVES 4

FOR THE BEAN SAUCE:

2 tablespoons vegetable oil

½ large white onion, minced

2 garlic cloves, minced

3 cups drained Refried Beans (page 49) or canned black beans, drained and rinsed

¾ cup unsweetened coconut milk

1 teaspoon kosher salt

TO FINISH:

½ cup vegetable oil

12 store-bought corn tortillas

½ cup crumbled queso fresco

½ large white onion, very thinly sliced

TOTAL COOK TIME

45 minutes

"DROWNED" EGGS IN COCONUT SAUCE
(Huevos Ahogados en Salsa de Coco)

Ahogados means "drowned," and eggs that have been "drowned" in a mild chile sauce are a typical Veracruzano breakfast. Here, we take inspiration from Thai restaurants—as well as the ubiquity of coconuts in Veracruz—and add coconut cream to the sauce. There are many similarities between Mexican cooking and traditional Thai food. Coconut cream, which adds flavor, texture, and richness to tomato-based stews and seafood soups, is a common ingredient in recipes from both cultures. Be sure to use unsweetened coconut cream, and not the milk substitute called "coconut milk" or "lite" coconut cream, both of which are too watery. In cans of unsweetened coconut milk, there is often a thicker portion that rises to the top; this can also be used here.

1. In a large, deep skillet, heat the oil over medium-high heat. Add the garlic and stir for 30 seconds, then add the tomatoes, onion, mushrooms, jalapeño, salt, pepper, and bay leaves. Fry for 3 to 5 minutes, until the onion is translucent, the tomatoes have broken down, and the mushrooms have released some of their moisture. Add 1 cup water and the coconut cream and stir for 30 seconds. Taste the sauce and add more salt, if needed.

2. Very gently, crack the eggs one at a time in a single layer, so they sit atop the sauce. Turn the heat down to low, cover the pan, and cook for about 6 minutes, depending on how well-done you prefer your eggs. Serve immediately, garnished with the cilantro.

SERVES 4

2 tablespoons extra-virgin olive oil

12 garlic cloves, minced

1 pound very ripe Roma tomatoes (about 8), diced

1 large white onion, diced (about 1½ cups)

4 ounces cremini or button mushrooms, sliced (about 1 cup)

1 jalapeño chile, stemmed and thinly sliced

1 teaspoon kosher salt

1 teaspoon freshly ground black pepper

2 dried bay leaves

¼ cup unsweetened coconut cream

8 large eggs

¼ packed cup fresh cilantro leaves, minced

TOTAL COOK TIME

30 minutes

TIPS

These are especially good served with Refried Beans (page 49) and freshly made Corn Tortillas (page 39) for breakfast or brunch.

To make this dish even heartier, stir 8 ounces diced queso fresco into the sauce just before adding the eggs.

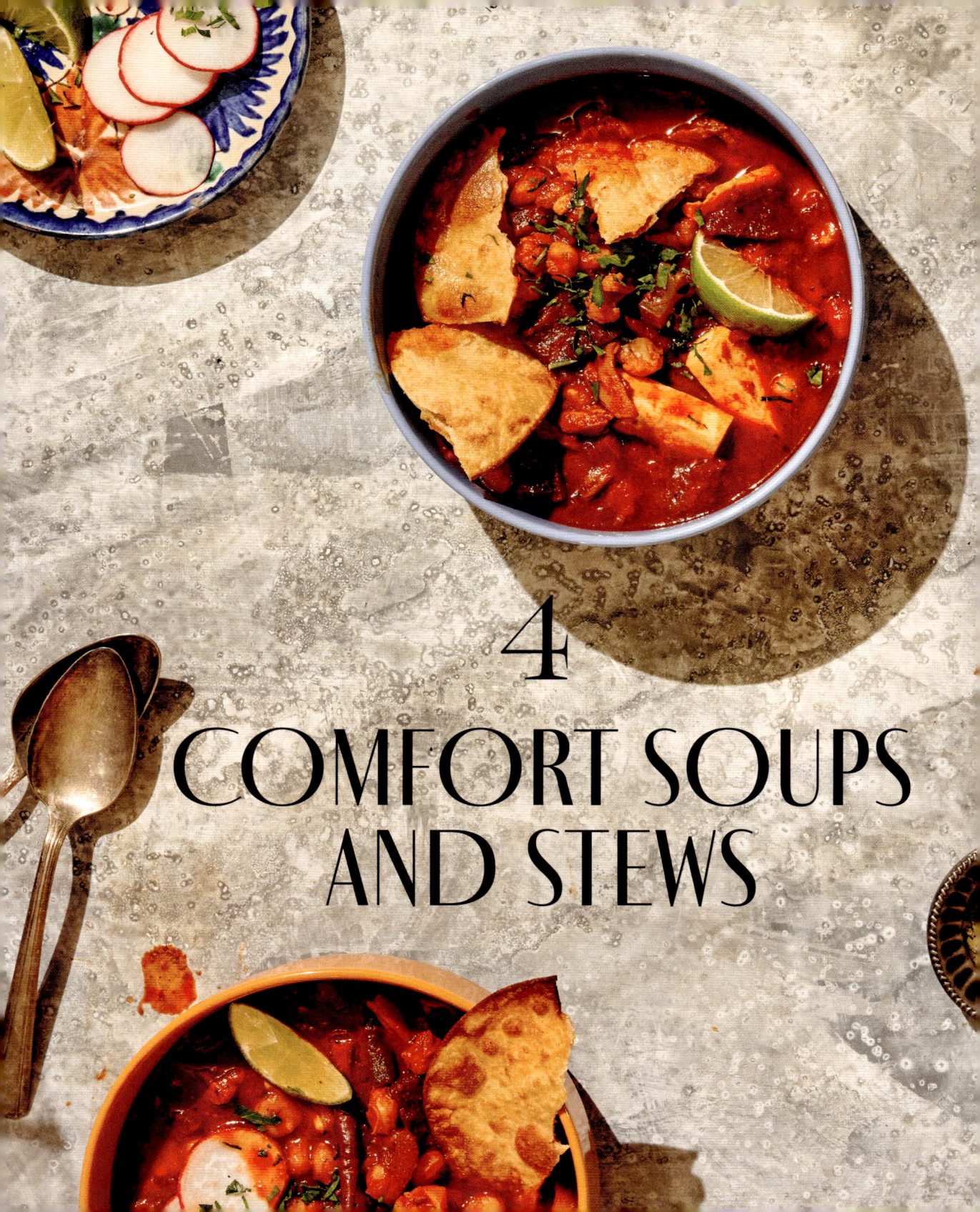

4

COMFORT SOUPS AND STEWS

"Del plato a la boca, se cae la sopa."

(FROM THE DISH TO THE MOUTH, THE SOUP SPILLS.)

Like "Don't count your chickens before they hatch," this saying is a reminder that life is uncertain.

NOTHING HAS EVER BEEN A certainty for us, and it still feels like it could all disappear at any moment. Our early years in Austin were challenging, trying to contribute to the city as business owners but without legal access to such basics as bank accounts, loans, and investors. Family and community saved us. New friends and volunteer organizations helped us with everything from childcare to fixing kitchen equipment. In turn, as we achieved some success and independence, giving back to our community has been a priority. Just as food kept our family close when life pulled it in unexpected directions, food has allowed us to contribute to causes that keep communities strong: women's rights, immigration, art, culture, mental health, domestic violence, education, and the environment.

We've donated portions of tacos sales to organizations like Posada Esperanza, which welcomes displaced immigrants and promotes self-sufficiency by providing shelter and support services for immigrant mothers escaping domestic or cultural violence. We often open up our spaces for fundraising and cultural events. For example, we partner with Esquina Tango to host its salsa nights at our East Austin location, and we work with Sana Yoga, which provides Latino and other marginalized communities with inclusive spaces to practice yoga; it also offers other physical and mental health resources. We were honored to be keynote speakers for Startup Chica, an entrepreneurial conference for Latinas between the ages of nine and fourteen.

When we closed our businesses during the COVID pandemic, we provided furloughed employees with fresh produce and other kitchen basics. During the historic Central Texas snowstorm of 2021, we gave away almost five thousand tacos from our location at the Line hotel and delivered meals to local hospitals, schools, community centers, and first responders. We will always continue to pay it forward as long as we can.

All of which feels apt to introduce this chapter, which is about comfort food. With most of our extended family back in Veracruz, and until recently unable to leave the country to visit them, our Austin community *is* family, and family equals comfort. For us "soup" is a hearty one-pot meal that exudes warmth and coziness year-round. These recipes are roughly organized from lighter to heartier, but all are generous and flavorful enough to be the centerpiece of anything from a casual lunch to a celebratory feast.

FAVA BEAN SOUP
(Sopa de Habas)

At home, our mom would make this recipe as a main dish. We loved eating it with tortillas, ripping them into pieces and soaking them in the soup to make it even heartier. The best part was when she'd cook down the leftover soup the next day into a thick puree to make tostadas de haba, topped with more onion, cilantro, cheese, and salsa. You can also poach eggs in the leftover soup the next morning for a particularly protein-packed breakfast. Double this recipe if you think you'll be craving leftovers.

In a stockpot or Dutch oven, combine the habas, salt, and 3½ quarts water. Bring to a boil over high heat, then partly cover the pot and cook until the habas are very soft and some are starting to fall apart, 45 minutes to 60 minutes (see Tip). Add more water or let some water evaporate, as needed, to achieve a thick, comforting soupy texture. Taste and season with more salt, if needed. Just before serving, turn the heat down to low, stir in the onion and cilantro, and let simmer for 5 minutes.

SERVES 4 TO 6

1 pound (about 3 cups) habas (dried peeled fava beans)

1 tablespoon kosher salt

1 large white onion, diced

1 packed cup minced fresh cilantro leaves

TOTAL COOK TIME

1½ hours

TIP

Different brands of dried habas vary widely in terms of how long they take to cook, so be sure to allot enough time in case yours take closer to an hour, or even more.

VERACRUZANO CRAB SOUP
(Chilpachole de Jaiba)

For most of our childhood, our dad drove a little Volkswagen bug. There was room for five of us and a bucket. During crab season, we'd drive to the beach late at night when the crabs came out to walk along the beach and even on the streets. Dad would pull over on the side of the road and, with thick cloth gloves, just toss them in the bucket. It was a thrill for us to get these full-size crabs for free, picturing the delicious chilpachole de jaiba that our mom would make for us the following day.

One of the glories of Mexican cooking is that it doesn't rely on meats and fats to flavor sauces, soups, and stews. Chiles, vegetables, and herbs play this role, and stirring a simple blended salsa into a broth can make a soup taste like it's been simmering for hours. This recipe is simply our seafood stock combined with a quick tomato-chile salsa, thickened with masa, and made hearty with crabs and shrimp. The result is one of the most iconic soups of Veracruz, equally at home in a humble fonda as in the country's finest restaurants. Serve with White Rice (page 46), fresh tortillas, and lime wedges.

1. In a medium saucepan, add the tomatoes and chiles de árbol and pour in enough water to cover them by 1 inch. Bring to a boil over high heat and cook for 15 minutes. Drain and transfer the tomatoes and chiles to a blender, along with the garlic, masa (dough), salt, and 2 cups water. Blend until smooth.

2. In a Dutch oven or stockpot, heat the oil over medium-high heat. Add the paprika and tomato mixture and cook, stirring constantly, for 2 minutes. Add the seafood broth and stir until smooth, then add the crabs and epazote, if using. Cook for 15 minutes, then taste and add more salt, if needed. Add the shrimp and cook for about 5 minutes, or just until the shrimp are cooked through.

3. To serve, divide the crabs and shrimp among bowls and ladle the broth on top.

SERVES 4 TO 6

6 Roma tomatoes

5 chiles de árbol, stemmed

6 large garlic cloves, peeled

½ cup Corn Tortilla Dough (page 38)

1 teaspoon kosher salt

¼ cup vegetable oil

1 teaspoon paprika

12 cups Seafood Broth (page 56) or store-bought

2½ pounds whole blue crabs, cleaned and halved (see Tip for alternatives)

4 fresh epazote sprigs (optional but strongly recommended)

1 pound large head-on shrimp, unpeeled

TOTAL COOK TIME

1 hour

TIP

Though blue crab is most common in Veracruz, this dish can be made with Dungeness crab clusters or cracked snow crab legs, or with any combination of white fish (such as snapper), shrimp, lobster, or langoustines.

LENTILS WITH PLANTAIN AND CHORIZO
(Lentejas Veracruzanas)

Meaty, sweet, and earthy, this lentil preparation, which is common in Veracruz and southern Mexico, is somewhere between a soup and a stew. It is a terrific one-pot meal, more satisfying than even the heartiest lentil soup. Ripe plantains are key to this dish. A ripe plantain is mostly black with some yellow spots. Like bananas, plantains will ripen on the kitchen counter, but they will ripen faster if your kitchen is around 75°F.

1. In a large saucepan, bring 4 quarts water and the salt to a boil. Add the lentils, partly cover the pan, and boil for 20 minutes, then remove from the heat.

2. While the lentils cook, in a blender, combine the tomatoes, onion, garlic, and $\frac{1}{3}$ cup water. Blend until smooth, then set aside.

3. In a large skillet, heat the oil over high heat. Add the plantains in a single layer and cook until they are a deep golden brown on both sides, 2 to 3 minutes per side. Transfer the plantains to a paper towel–lined plate and discard the oil, but do not wipe out the pan.

4. Add the bacon to the same pan and cook over medium heat for about 3 minutes, or until it starts to render fat and turn translucent. Add the chorizo and cook for about another 3 minutes, stirring to break up the meat, or until the chorizo is cooked through. Add the tomato mixture, scraping up any browned bits. Set aside.

5. Return the lentils to high heat and add the plantains, meat mixture, bay leaves, and jalapeño. Continue boiling, uncovered, for about 10 minutes, or until the lentils are very soft. Taste and add more salt, if needed. Serve hot, in shallow bowls.

SERVES 4 TO 6

1 tablespoon kosher salt

1 pound (about 2¼ cups) lentils, rinsed

4 Roma tomatoes, halved

1 small white onion, chopped

2 garlic cloves, peeled

½ cup vegetable oil

2 ripe plantains, peeled and cut diagonally into ½-inch slices

1 cup chopped thin-sliced bacon (about 8 ounces)

1 cup Mexican chorizo (about 8 ounces), removed from casing

3 dried bay leaves

1 jalapeño chile, stemmed and halved lengthwise

TOTAL COOK TIME

1 hour

GREEN "POT MOLE" WITH BEEF
(Mole de Olla Verde)

Epazote and hoja santa are two distinctive Mexican herbs for which there are no substitutes. Epazote smells like an earthy cross between oregano and mint, and is commonly paired with beans. Hoja santa is sometimes called "root beer plant" in the US for its sarsaparilla-like taste. The dried versions of these herbs are essentially flavorless, so we recommend making this recipe only when you can find fresh epazote and hoja santa (luckily, they're becoming easier to find in Mexican markets). The quantities of cilantro, epazote, and hoja santa here are intentionally approximate; as you make this dish repeatedly, you might find you prefer more or less of these wonderfully pungent herbs.

That said, when you *do* find these herbs, this is the first recipe you should make. There are countless versions of mole de olla (which is more like a soup than the thick, sweet sauce most people think of when they see the word *mole*) in Mexico, but the green ones are the best. They're lighter with less fat, and they're full of vegetables; the beef is there just for flavor. Our favorite part is the little masa dumplings, which we call ombliguitos ("little belly buttons"); the flavor reminds us of tamales. In the winter, we make this dish a lot, adding rice to soak in the broth. We also include tortillas that have been heated over an open flame so that they char a little, giving a slight smokiness to each bite of stew. Having leftovers is never a problem because this tastes even better when it's reheated.

RECIPE CONTINUES

SERVES 6

FOR THE OMBLIGUITOS:

1 cup Corn Tortilla Dough (page 38)

2 tablespoons coconut oil (cold), pork lard (cold), or butter (room temperature)

½ teaspoon kosher salt

FOR THE SALSA:

7 medium tomatillos, husked and rinsed

4 serrano chiles, stemmed

4 garlic cloves, peeled

¼ medium white onion

½ packed cup fresh cilantro leaves and stems

1 handful epazote leaves (about 10)

1 large hoja santa leaf (about 10 inches across)

½ teaspoon kosher salt

FOR THE MOLE:

3 pounds cross-cut beef shank or oxtail (at least 6 pieces)

2 tablespoons kosher salt

6 garlic cloves, peeled

¼ medium white onion, chopped

6 small new potatoes or 3 small red potatoes, halved

1 large zucchini, peeled and cut crosswise into 6 pieces

1 large carrot, peeled and cut crosswise into 6 pieces

1 teaspoon dried oregano

½ packed cup fresh cilantro leaves and stems

½ head cabbage, cored and cut into 6 equal pieces

2 ears fresh corn, shucked and cut crosswise into 3 pieces

TOTAL COOK TIME

2 hours

1. To make the ombliguitos, in a large bowl, mix the masa (dough), coconut oil, and salt with your hands until well combined—the more you mix, the lighter the ombliguitos will be. (Alternatively, you can use a stand mixer fitted with the paddle attachment.) Roll the dough into balls about 1 inch diameter and make an indentation with your finger to create a tiny bowl shape. Cover and refrigerate until ready to use.

2. To make the salsa, in a blender, place the tomatillos, serranos, garlic, onion, cilantro, epazote, hoja santa, salt, and 1 cup water and blend until smooth. Set aside.

3. To make the mole, in a large stockpot, combine the beef, salt, and 3 quarts water and bring to a boil over high heat. Once boiling, skim any foam that comes to the surface, and add the garlic and onion. Partly cover the pot and cook over high heat for 45 minutes (the liquid should reduce by about half).

4. To the stockpot, add another 3 quarts water, plus the salsa, potatoes, zucchini, carrot, oregano, and cilantro. Cook, uncovered, for about 15 minutes, or until the potatoes are soft. Add the cabbage and corn, stir to mix, then carefully add the ombliguitos. Cook for another 4 minutes. Serve in large soup bowls, with a piece of beef at the bottom, vegetables divided evenly, and plenty of ombliguitos for everyone.

CREAMED CORN
(Crema de Elote)

We grew up harvesting corn in our backyard, and we ate everything we could with corn. This version of creamed corn was always a favorite. As adults, it's been a goal to make our favorite recipes a little healthier, and this is a good example. If anything, it's even more delicious than the one we made as kids.

Think of this recipe as the basis for your own preferred version. It can be made completely vegan by eliminating the butter, or substitute chicken broth for the vegetable broth, or use Mexican crema instead of the coconut cream.

1. In a stockpot or Dutch oven, heat the butter and oil over high heat. Once the butter has melted, add the onion, garlic, and the minced serrano and cook until the onion is translucent, about 2 minutes. Add the fresh corn and cook, stirring often, for 5 minutes. Add the broth, bring to a boil for 2 minutes, then remove the pot from the heat.

2. Transfer the corn mixture to a blender, in batches if needed, along with the salt, pepper, oregano, and epazote, if using. Blend the mixture until it is smooth, then return it to the pot over medium heat. Add the coconut cream, cilantro sprig, and bay leaves and cook until it is heated through and bubbly. Stir in the grilled corn, if using, just before serving. Garnish with the sliced serrano and minced cilantro.

SERVES 4 TO 8

4 tablespoons unsalted butter

2 tablespoons extra-virgin olive oil

½ large white onion, minced

6 garlic cloves, minced

1 serrano chile, stemmed, half minced and half sliced

4½ cups fresh or frozen corn kernels

2 cups Vegetable Broth (page 55) or store-bought

1 teaspoon kosher salt

½ teaspoon freshly ground black pepper

½ teaspoon dried oregano

1 fresh epazote sprig (optional)

⅔ cup coconut cream

1 fresh cilantro sprig, plus ¼ cup minced fresh cilantro leaves, for garnish

2 dried bay leaves

2 ears fresh corn, shucked, grilled, and kernels removed (optional)

TOTAL COOK TIME
25 minutes

WHITE BEAN STEW WITH BACON AND CHARD
(Potaje de Alubias con Tocino)

This recipe makes us nostalgic for our childhood in Veracruz. Growing up, we always ate dinner together, and this one-pot meal could feed the whole family affordably, with just a little bit of bacon adding flavor to the whole potaje, or stew. Some meals would last for hours, and we served ourselves seconds and thirds from the pot between laughter, chatter, and chisme (gossip).

Life in Austin is very fast-paced compared to Veracruz, and family dinners are not a regularity as they were back home, yet food is still the thing that brings us together. From time to time Mom calls us and our brother to say she's made this stew, and it's like a code phrase that means, "Come and re-create those childhood memories." Without fail, we all manage to show up over the potaje pot again.

1. In a large stockpot or Dutch oven, combine the beans, salt, and 5 quarts water. Partly cover the pot and bring to a boil over high heat. Boil for at least 1½ hours, until the beans are soft and creamy (different brands sometimes require different cooking times). If too much water evaporates, add a little more to maintain a soupy texture.

3. After the beans have cooked for about an hour, in a medium saucepan, add the tomatoes and chipotles and cover with water. Bring to a boil over high heat, then boil for 15 minutes. Using a slotted spoon, transfer the tomatoes and chiles to a blender. Add the onion and garlic and blend until smooth. Set aside.

3. When the beans are ready (they should mash easily with a spoon), uncover the pot and turn the heat down to a simmer. In a deep skillet, add the bacon and cook over medium-high heat, stirring occasionally, until the bacon releases its fat and starts to crisp, about 10 minutes. Add the tomato mixture, chard, and bay leaves (careful, it will splatter). Stir well to scrape up any browned bits, then add the contents of the pan to the pot of beans.

4. Cook the stew for about 10 minutes, adding more salt, if needed, and either adding more water if the beans seem dry or letting some water evaporate to thicken. You want a hearty "stew" texture. Serve.

SERVES 6 TO 8

1 pound dried cannellini or navy beans

2 tablespoons kosher salt

3 Roma tomatoes

3 dried chipotle chiles, stemmed

¼ medium white onion

5 garlic cloves, peeled

5 ounces sliced bacon, chopped

1 bunch chard (about 12 ounces), chopped

2 dried bay leaves

Corn Tortillas (page 39) or storebought, for serving (optional)

TOTAL COOK TIME
2½ hours

TIP
Make the beans ahead of time (they will keep in a tightly covered container in the refrigerator for up to 4 days), and you can have this on the table in less than 30 minutes.

VEGETARIAN POZOLE
(Pozole Vegetariano)

It's been said (mostly by our family members and Mexican friends) that a great vegetarian pozole can't be done, but we've made converts of even our most carnivorous compatriots with this recipe. Our combination of spices, chiles, and other vegetables gives the same depth as the usual pork broth—maybe even more! As a bonus, this pozole comes together in far less time than the traditional pork version. We love how the queso fresco can be used as a primary protein source. The effect is almost like firm tofu, but with much better flavor. Queso fresco doesn't melt, but it gets very soft and the little bits that fall off enrich the sauce.

1. Roast the poblanos by placing them directly over a gas flame or under a broiler. Turn them often until the skin is blackened but not disintegrated. Place them in a ziplock bag or covered bowl for at least 5 minutes. When they are cool enough to handle, gently peel the charred skin (it's OK if some remains), then make a lengthwise slit and carefully remove the seeds, veins, and stem. Cut into ½-inch dice and set aside.

2. In a small skillet, toast the chiles de árbol over medium heat, tossing often, until they start to turn color and smell toasty, about 2 minutes. Set aside.

3. In a medium saucepan, combine the tomatoes, guajillos, and ancho with 4 cups water. Bring to a boil over high heat and cook for 10 minutes. Using tongs, transfer the tomatoes and chiles to a blender, then add ¼ cup of the cooking liquid. Add the garlic, chipotle chile, cloves, peppercorns, cumin seeds, and 1 teaspoon of the salt and blend until very smooth. Add more cooking liquid, if needed, to keep the blades turning. Set aside.

4. In a Dutch oven or heavy saucepan, heat the oil over medium heat. Add the celery, onion, and remaining 1 teaspoon salt and cook for about 3 minutes, or until soft and translucent. Add the roasted poblanos, red bell pepper, and oyster mushrooms and cook, stirring often, for another 2 minutes. Add the cauliflower, hominy, and blended sauce and cook for another 3 minutes. Add the broth, queso fresco, toasted chiles de árbol, bay leaves, and oregano and cook, stirring occasionally, for 12 minutes longer. Add additional vegetable broth if too much liquid cooks away (it should be like a brothy stew). Taste and add more salt, if needed. Ladle the soup into bowls and serve, advising guests not to eat the whole árbol chiles and bay leaves.

SERVES 6

3 poblano chiles

12 chiles de árbol, stemmed

4 Roma tomatoes

8 guajillo chiles, stemmed and seeded

1 ancho chile, stemmed and seeded

8 garlic cloves, peeled

1 canned chipotle chile in adobo

5 whole cloves

¼ teaspoon black peppercorns

¼ teaspoon cumin seeds

2 teaspoons kosher salt, divided

3 tablespoons extra-virgin olive oil

2 cups diced celery

1 cup diced red onion

1⅓ cups minced red bell pepper

8 ounces oyster or portobello mushrooms, torn into 1-inch pieces

2 cups cauliflower (roughly 1-inch pieces)

1 (29-ounce) can or 2 (15-ounce) cans Goya white hominy, drained

4 cups Vegetable Broth (page 55) or store-bought

2 cups queso fresco, cut into 1-inch cubes

4 dried bay leaves

1 teaspoon dried oregano

TOTAL COOK TIME

1 hour

TIP

For a vegan pozole, replace the cheese with firm tofu or a firm, unsliced vegan cheese substitute.

CHICKEN AND VEGETABLE STEW
(Puchero de Pollo y Verduras)

Puchero is way better than "regular" chicken soup, and it is what Mama Reyna would cook for us when we got sick. The rice absorbs flavor from the broth, and the charred notes of the salsa add depth. While boneless, skinless chicken make this a light and clean-tasting soup that allows the vegetables' flavors to shine through, our mom would sometimes add chicken feet, wings, and even livers or gizzards to the soup to add nutrition and feed more people. Make this recipe with whatever chicken parts you enjoy. This dish has it all—protein, rice, comfort, spiciness—and it's just plain delicious.

1. Using a comal, wire rack, or steel steamer basket (see Tatemado, page 70) set over a high-heat gas flame, cook the tomatoes, 2 unpeeled garlic cloves, and the chiles de árbol until everything is blackened all over but not yet turning to ash. The tomatoes and garlic cloves will take about 2 minutes and the chiles just 10 seconds, or until fragrant. As each piece blackens, transfer to a plate. Add the charred vegetables to a blender, along with ½ cup water, and blend until smooth. Set aside.

2. In a large stockpot or Dutch oven, add the chicken, the remaining 6 garlic cloves, the onion, salt, and 3 quarts water. Partly cover the pot and cook over high heat for 40 minutes, skimming off any foam that rises to the surface. Using tongs, transfer the chicken to a plate. If using bone-in chicken, you can remove the meat and discard the bones; we usually leave the pieces intact. With a slotted spoon, remove and discard the garlic and onion from the pot, leaving the broth.

3. Add another 12 cups water to the pot, along with the rice, potatoes, corn, zucchini, carrot, jalapeños, oregano, and blended salsa. Cook over medium-high heat for about 20 minutes, or until the potatoes are soft and the rice is fully cooked. Add the cabbage and shredded chicken and cook for another 4 minutes, adding more salt or other seasonings, if needed. Divide the vegetables and chicken equally among bowls. Serve with cilantro, onion, and limes passed separately.

SERVES 6

4 Roma tomatoes

8 garlic cloves, 2 unpeeled, and 6 peeled

3 chiles de árbol, stemmed

1 pound boneless, skinless chicken breasts or thighs or 1½ pounds bone-in, skinless chicken parts

¼ medium white onion

1½ tablespoons kosher salt

1 cup long-grain rice

2 large red potatoes, cut into 3 pieces

2 ears fresh corn, shucked and cut crosswise into 3 pieces

1 large zucchini, cut crosswise into 6 pieces

1 large carrot, peeled and cut crosswise into 6 pieces

2 jalapeño chiles, stemmed and quartered lengthwise

1 teaspoon dried oregano

½ head green cabbage, cored and cut into 4 pieces

½ packed cup chopped fresh cilantro leaves

½ packed cup minced red onion

2 limes, cut into wedges

TOTAL COOK TIME
1½ hours

TIP
Serve this recipe with tortillas that have been heated over a fire until charred for guests to tear and soak in the soup.

MEXICAN-STYLE PASTA WITH CHICKEN
(Sopa de Fideo Seco con Pollo)

Fideo is essentially cut angel hair pasta, found in every market in Mexico, and every Mexican home cook has a recipe for preparing it. It's usually sold in 7-ounce packages and is also easy to find in the US in any Mexican grocery and most larger supermarkets. Even though this is a noodle dish, it's in the category of Mexican dishes called sopa seca, or "dry soup" (rice cooked in broth is also considered a sopa seca). Though fideo seco is often served before a main course, we like making it a full main dish, as here.

1. In a large saucepan, combine the chicken, salt, half of the onion, and 3 quarts water. Bring to a boil over high heat and cook for 15 minutes. Strain through a strainer set over a large bowl, and reserve the chicken pieces and chicken broth separately. Discard the onion.

2. Meanwhile, in a blender, combine the remaining onion, tomatoes, garlic, and tomato paste and blend until smooth. Set aside.

3. In a wide stockpot or deep, heavy skillet, heat the oil over medium-high heat. Add the fideos and cook, stirring often, until they turn golden brown, about 4 minutes. Add the tomato mixture and cook, stirring often, for 3 minutes. Add $4\frac{1}{2}$ cups of the reserved chicken broth, the cilantro, and jalapeños, and stir well. Place the chicken pieces on top, cover, turn the heat to low, and cook until the liquid is absorbed, about 10 minutes. Stir every few minutes to make sure it's not sticking. Serve immediately, reserving any leftover noodles for Stir-Fry Mexicano (page 139).

SERVES 6

$2\frac{1}{2}$ pounds bone-in, skinless chicken thighs or other chicken parts

1 tablespoon kosher salt

1 medium white onion, roughly chopped, divided

6 Roma tomatoes, quartered

2 garlic cloves, peeled

2 tablespoons tomato paste

2 tablespoons extra-virgin olive oil

2 (7-ounce) packages fideos

$\frac{3}{4}$ packed cup fresh cilantro leaves, chopped roughly

2 jalapeño chiles, stemmed

TOTAL COOK TIME
45 minutes

TIP
If you can't find fideos, you can use a 1-pound package of angel hair pasta, broken into roughly 3-inch pieces.

STIR-FRY MEXICANO

When we make Mexican-Style Pasta with Chicken (page 138), there are usually some noodles left over. We use the leftovers to make a Mexican-inspired stir-fry as a quick lunch for one or two people. You can use any firm chopped vegetables here, such as broccoli, cauliflower, green beans, zucchini, or bell peppers.

Place a wok or skillet over high heat for about a minute, then swirl in the oil. Add the garlic and let it brown for a few seconds. Add the mushrooms, carrot, and asparagus and cook, stirring often, until the vegetables are cooked through but still a little firm, about 4 minutes depending on the vegetable type and size. Add the fideos, serrano (if using), and 1/4 cup water. Stir to mix the noodles thoroughly, about 1 minute. Salt to taste and serve immediately.

SERVES 1 TO 2

1 tablespoon extra-virgin olive oil

3 garlic cloves, minced

1/2 cup quartered button mushrooms

1/2 cup sliced carrot

2 asparagus stalks, each cut into 6 pieces

1 cup (or more) leftover noodles from Mexican-Style Pasta with Chicken (page 138)

1/2 serrano chile, stemmed and thinly sliced (optional)

Kosher salt

TOTAL COOK TIME

15 minutes

5

VEGETABLES IN THE MIDDLE OF THE PLATE

"Si tomas tequila y comes verduras tendrás las nalgas bien duras."

(IF YOU DRINK TEQUILA AND EAT VEGETABLES, YOU'LL HAVE A FIRM BUTT.)

We can't guarantee the firm butt, but as the adage suggests, nothing bad can come from a daily dose of vegetables.

NEITHER OF US IS STRICTLY vegetarian, but we try to maintain a healthy diet, which means eating lots of vegetables and limiting meat. At our restaurants, it's extremely important to us that our menus welcome people of all dietary needs, restrictions, beliefs, and desires. Many of our salsas, sides, and snacks are vegan, and many other recipes in this book can easily be made vegetarian. We often replace meat not just with root vegetables and brassicas (cabbage, cauliflower, broccoli), but also with poblano chiles, mushrooms, greens, beans, eggs, and queso fresco. While there are plenty of other vegetarian recipes in this book, this chapter is a collection of hearty entrées where vegetables take center stage—some are traditional in Veracruz, and some are our vegetarian adaptations of favorite Veracruzano dishes.

Growing up, we never really thought of our diets as "healthy" because what we ate was born out of necessity. In Veracruz, what was cheapest was what was local, seasonal, and abundant—namely, vegetables and seafood. It was something of a shock to come to the US and find that the cheapest food was processed, mass-produced, and from fast-food chains. Buying local and seasonal vegetables is largely considered a luxury. The farmers markets here are amazing, and not dissimilar to how we shopped in Veracruz, but the prices make them out of reach for much of the population.

When we arrived in Austin, we quickly realized that we had to adapt our diets to maintain our health while dealing with extremely busy schedules and extremely limited incomes. It's always easiest to cook what is fast and easy, but that doesn't have to mean cutting corners or using premade ingredients. Vegetables are a solution to all of this. Even organic and farmers market vegetables cost less than good-quality meat. And compared to meat, they keep longer, cook quickly, and adapt to almost any sauce or technique.

Before the Spanish brought domesticated animals (chicken, pigs, cattle, etc.) and dairy, Mexicans ate primarily corn, beans, chiles, squash, avocados, tomatoes, tomatillos, greens, and cactus, and those are still core ingredients to us. We know there's demand for more vegetables in Mexican restaurants: When we worked as servers, people would always ask if we could add spinach or other vegetables to dishes, use vegetable fillings in enchiladas and burritos, and substitute vegetables for rice, which is largely how we developed our taco lineup for our taco trucks.

We want to reclaim the vegetable focus of traditional Mexican cuisine. Join us!

ZUCCHINI AND CHEESE
(Calabacitas con Queso)

This quick but satisfying dish defines comida casera—homestyle cooking—for us. It's a staple of our childhood, and when creating the menu for our first dine-in restaurant, Veracruz Fonda & Bar, we knew this had to be an always-available vegetarian entrée. It shows how versatile vegetables can be, and it is appealing to guests of all ages. We serve it with black or refried black beans, rice, plantains, and tortillas. Putting everything together in a taco makes for the perfect bite. If you don't have beans, plantains, and tortillas, serve it with White Rice (page 46) or Mexican Rice (page 47).

The queso fresco will become soft when heated, but it doesn't melt, making it an interesting protein to use in place of meat, seafood, or tofu. It adds great flavor and texture to this surprisingly complex zucchini stir-fry.

1. Using a comal, a wire rack, or a steel steamer basket (see Tatemado, page 70) set over a high-heat gas flame or on a rimmed baking sheet in a single layer under a broiler at the highest settting, char the zucchini. When it's speckled with black spots, transfer to a plate. This step improves both flavor and texture. If using fresh corn, sear it in the same way and cut from the cob.

2. In a large skillet, heat the butter and oil over high heat. When it starts to sizzle and smell nutty, add the zucchini, cheese, garlic, and 1 teaspoon of the salt. Cook, stirring occasionally, for about 4 minutes, to soften the cheese and zucchini slightly (it's OK if the cheese breaks up a little, but you don't want the zucchini to turn to mush).

3. Add the jalapeño, tomato, onion, corn, pepper, and the remaining 1 teaspoon salt and cook for another 5 minutes, stirring often, until both the onion and zucchini are soft. Serve right away.

SERVES 4

3 large zucchini, or summer squash, cut into 1-inch chunks

¾ cup fresh or frozen corn kernels (from about 1 ear)

3 tablespoons unsalted butter

1 tablespoon vegetable oil

10 ounces queso fresco, cut into thumb-size chunks

5 garlic cloves, minced

2 teaspoons kosher salt, divided

1 jalapeño chile, stemmed and sliced

1 Roma tomato, diced

1 small white onion, diced

1½ teaspoons freshly ground black pepper

TOTAL COOK TIME

30 minutes

TIP

To make this dish vegan, substitute firm tofu for the cheese and add a little coconut cream for creaminess and a hint of sweetness.

MUSHROOM CARNITAS
(Carnitas de Hongos)

Using mushrooms as a meat substitute is familiar to most people, but here the mushrooms don't try to mimic the pork that's traditionally used in carnitas. Instead, they combine crisp edges with tender cores in a marinade that highlights the mushrooms' deep earthy flavor. And, of course, this dish comes together in a fraction of the time of traditional carnitas. If you can't find oyster mushrooms, substitute portobellos.

1. In a blender, combine the garlic, onion, beer, orange juice, evaporated milk, lime juice, vinegar, salt, sugar, soy, thyme, oregano, and peppercorns. Blend until smooth. Transfer the mixture to a large bowl and add the mushrooms, tossing to coat. Marinate for at least 1 hour at room temperature or up to 24 hours in the refrigerator.

2. In a wok or very large, deep skillet, heat the oil over high heat. Remove the mushrooms from the marinade, shaking off and discarding the excess marinade, and add them to the skillet. Cook, stirring often, until they start to brown and release liquid, about 5 minutes. Add the reserved orange half (the peel releases flavor) and keep frying until the mushrooms are soft and there is no more liquid left in the pan, about 5 minutes longer. Add salt, if needed, and remove and discard the orange half. Serve immediately with tortillas, cilantro, onion, and salsa.

SERVES 4

4 garlic cloves, peeled

2 tablespoons chopped white onion

2 tablespoons IPA beer

2 tablespoons freshly squeezed orange juice (reserve 1 squeezed orange half)

2 tablespoons evaporated milk

1 teaspoon freshly squeezed lime juice

1 teaspoon apple cider vinegar

1 teaspoon kosher salt

1 teaspoon brown sugar

1 teaspoon soy sauce

¼ teaspoon dried thyme

¼ teaspoon dried oregano

¼ teaspoon black peppercorns

1¼ pounds oyster mushrooms, wiped clean with a paper towel and torn into rough 1-inch squares

¼ cup extra-virgin olive oil

Corn Tortillas (page 39) or store-bought, fresh cilantro, chopped white onion, and Raw Green Salsa (page 95), for serving

TOTAL COOK TIME

20 minutes, plus 1 hour marinating time

TIP

Coconut milk can be used in place of the evaporated milk to make this dish vegan.

CAULIFLOWER "AL PASTOR"
(Coliflor al Pastor)

The idea for this dish is pretty straightforward: Create a vegan version of tacos al pastor, which are typically made with sliced pork. Traditional flavors like guajillo chile and pineapple give the sauce a perfect sweet-savory balance, and frying the cauliflower gives this dish a deep flavor and a firm texture. Creamy refried beans aren't typically served with tacos al pastor, but they are perfect here.

1. In a small saucepan, combine the guajillos with just enough water to cover them, and bring to a boil. Cook for 10 minutes. Using tongs or a slotted spoon, transfer the chiles to a blender, along with the onion, pineapple, garlic, paprika, salt, and pepper. Puree until very smooth, for at least 2 minutes to break down the chile skins. Add a little of the chile water, if needed, to help turn the blades.

2. In a large, deep skillet (it will eventually hold the cauliflower), heat 1 tablespoon oil over medium heat. Add all the sauce (careful, it will splatter) and cook, stirring occasionally, for 1 minute. Remove from the heat. Spoon out half of the salsa and reserve for another use; it will keep in a tightly covered container in the refrigerator for up to 1 week.

3. In a large, heavy pot or Dutch oven, add oil to a depth of 2 inches. Heat the oil over medium-high heat to 350°F. Add the cauliflower in batches and fry, turning occasionally to cook evenly, until golden brown and crispy, about 5 minutes total. As the cauliflower cooks, use a slotted spoon or spider strainer to transfer the florets to a paper towel–lined plate or baking sheet. When they are all cooked, reheat the skillet of salsa over medium heat and add the cauliflower to coat and warm through.

4. Serve with hot tortillas and the other garnishes for guests to make their own tacos.

SERVES 4 TO 8

10 guajillo chiles, stemmed and seeded

2 tablespoons chopped white onion

½ cup diced fresh pineapple

4 garlic cloves, peeled

1½ teaspoons paprika

1 teaspoon kosher salt

½ teaspoon freshly ground black pepper

Vegetable oil, for frying

2 cauliflower heads, cut into florets about 3 inches long and 2 inches across

FOR SERVING:

Corn Tortillas (page 39) or store-bought

1 cup minced white onion

1 cup minced fresh cilantro leaves

1 cup minced fresh pineapple (charred on a grill first, ideally)

2 cups Refried Beans (page 49)

Creamy Jalapeño Salsa (page 73) (optional)

TOTAL COOK TIME

1 hour

ROASTED CAULIFLOWER IN CHARRED VEGETABLE SAUCE
(Coliflor Rostizada en Salsa Tatemada)

Our mom used to make battered deep-fried cauliflower in sauce for us when we were little, and it was one of our favorite dishes. We would get as excited watching her cut up cauliflower as we would looking at desserts or candy (yes, really). As adults, we wanted to make something that would not be as heavy, and a little healthier. By charring both the cauliflower and the vegetables (instead of frying them) for the sauce, a smoky flavor permeates this dish that brings it to another level.

1. Using a comal, a wire rack, or a steel steamer basket (see Tatemado, page 70) set over a high-heat gas flame, roast the 6 unpeeled garlic cloves, tomatoes, and serranos until they are charred on all sides, about 5 minutes total. Remove from the heat and when cool enough to handle, peel the garlic, discarding the skins. Add the garlic and chiles to a food processor, along with the salt, and blend until they almost become a paste. Add the tomatoes and $1/4$ cup water and pulse until combined but still chunky. Taste and add more salt, if needed.

2. In a comal or large skillet, over medium-high heat, add the cauliflower and cook, turning the pieces occasionally, until they are charred in spots and tender, about 10 minutes total. Transfer to a plate.

3. In a wide, deep skillet, melt the butter and add the minced garlic over medium heat. Add the cauliflower using tongs to coat the pieces on all sides. Let it cook, soaking up the butter, for 2 to 3 minutes, turning it occasionally.

4. Add the salsa to the pan with $1/2$ cup water and, using tongs or a spoon to coat the cauliflower, heat the sauce until it bubbles. Add the queso fresco, nudging it around so it's nestled in the sauce and not sitting on top of the cauliflower. Let the cheese heat through for about 1 minute, add salt to taste, if needed, and serve immediately.

SERVES 4

8 garlic cloves, 6 unpeeled and 2 peeled and minced

4 Roma tomatoes

2 serrano chiles, stemmed

1 teaspoon kosher salt

1 large whole cauliflower, stem trimmed, cut into 8 equal wedges

4 tablespoons unsalted butter

8 ounces queso fresco, cut into $1/2$-inch cubes

TOTAL COOK TIME

45 minutes

TIP

Feel free to try this recipe with some of the other cooked salsas in the book, such as Creamy Jalapeño Salsa (page 73), Chile de Árbol Salsa (page 74), and "Drunken" Salsa (page 66).

FOLDED ENCHILADAS
(Enchiladas Dobladas)

These quick enchiladas are essentially just tacos in sauce, but somehow they feel more festive and "complete" than a plate of tacos. Unlike the typical heavy, cheesy enchilada platters in Texas, traditional Mexican enchiladas are simply tortillas—filled, topped, or both—coated in chile salsa. Similarly, entomatadas are tortillas with tomato salsa, enmoladas are tortillas with mole, Enfrijoladas (page 113) are tortillas with a smooth bean sauce . . . you get the picture. Feel free to replace the salsa in this recipe with any cooked salsa you like. Round out the meal with White Rice (page 46).

1. In a medium skillet, add the salsa and keep warm over medium-low heat.

2. In another medium skillet, heat the oil over medium-high heat. Test the oil by dipping the edge of a tortilla into it; if it sizzles, it's hot enough. Using tongs, dip the tortillas in the oil one at a time for just 30 to 45 seconds—long enough for them to be pliable without breaking, but not long enough that they start to get hard (you may want to practice with one or two extra tortillas).

3. As you fry them, shake any excess oil back into the pan, then stack the tortillas on a plate (don't worry about any excess oil that sticks to them). When all the tortillas are fried, dunk them one at a time in the salsa to coat both sides, then transfer them to a plate. Add about 3 tablespoons filling to each and fold them in half. Repeat until there are 3 enchiladas on each plate. Cover with a little more salsa and garnish with lettuce, crema, and queso fresco, in that order. Serve immediately.

SERVES 4

3 cups Cooked Tomato Salsa (page 92) or Cooked Tomatillo Salsa (page 89)

½ cup vegetable oil

12 Corn Tortillas (page 39) or store-bought

3 cups cooked meat (such as ground or shredded beef, pork, or chicken) or vegetables (such as chopped steamed or grilled vegetables), hot or warm

½ head iceberg lettuce, shredded

½ cup Mexican crema

1 cup crumbled queso fresco (about 5 ounces)

TOTAL COOK TIME

30 minutes

CHAYOTE-POTATO SALAD
(Ensalada de Chayote y Papa)

Chayote has always been part of the Veracruz diet. It's in the same family as squash and melons and its taste and texture lie somewhere between zucchini and cucumber; like them, it is botanically a fruit that is culinarily considered a vegetable. You can eat every part of the vegetable from the skin to the seed. When we were kids, our mom would just boil them with a little salt; we'd split them open and scoop out the "meat" with a spoon. Our grandmother went a bit further, chopping them "a la mexicana"—with tomato, onion, and green chile—then stuffing them and topping them with breadcrumbs and cheese, and finishing them in the oven.

Mom's favorite way to cook chayote, though, was in this salad. We started bringing it to parties in Austin, and friends who had never cooked with chayote would ask for the recipe. Think of it as our version of a potluck potato salad. Chayotes are easy to find in Mexican markets and often in large supermarkets; kohlrabi makes an acceptable substitute in this dish, but otherwise wait to make this until you find fresh chayotes.

1. Bring a large pot of salted water to a boil. Add the chayotes and cook for 45 minutes. Add the potatoes and cook for 10 more minutes. Add the eggs and cook for 15 minutes longer. Drain and set the vegetables and eggs aside. When they are cool enough to handle, peel the chayotes, potatoes, and eggs. Cut the chayotes and potatoes into roughly 2-inch cubes and slice the eggs crosswise into 6 slices each.

2. In a large mixing bowl, whisk together the oil, vinegar, oregano, pepper, and salt to taste. Add the chayotes, potatoes, eggs, and onion, and toss gently. Add more salt and/or pepper to taste, if desired. Serve.

SERVES 4 TO 8

Kosher salt

1½ pounds chayotes (about 3), halved

1½ pounds white potatoes (about 4 medium), halved

3 large eggs

2 tablespoons extra-virgin olive oil

2 tablespoons apple cider vinegar

1 tablespoon dried oregano

¼ teaspoon freshly ground black pepper

½ medium white onion, very thinly sliced

TOTAL COOK TIME

2 hours

TIP

When buying chayotes, be sure they're firm and green, with no soft or brown spots.

CACTUS PADDLE SALAD
(Ensalada de Nopales)

The first time I (Reyna) tried this salad, I was a little girl walking in the mercado with my family. I was hesitant at first because it looked like the nopales were raw, and I'd only eaten cooked nopales. My mom insisted that I try it, and it soon became a favorite, especially for lunch when served on a tostada.

Some people are deterred by nopales because of their texture (which is similar to okra), but this salad is a great introduction to them with its zingy acidity, creamy queso fresco, and fresh raw veggies. Ensalada de nopales taught me to not be shy to try new things, and I hope it will encourage you to try nopales, too. Almost any market that sells fresh nopales will sell them cleaned, with the tiny thorns trimmed away.

SERVES 4 TO 8

1½ pounds fresh cleaned nopales (cactus paddles), trimmed and cut into ½-inch dice

1 small white onion, diced, divided

3 garlic cloves, peeled

2 tablespoons cider vinegar

1½ tablespoons kosher salt

½ teaspoon baking powder

1 pound Roma tomatoes, diced (about 2 cups)

¼ packed cup minced fresh cilantro leaves

3 tablespoons drained minced green chiles canned in vinegar, plus ¼ cup vinegar from the can

½ teaspoon freshly ground black pepper

8 ounces queso fresco, cut into ¼-inch dice

TOTAL COOK TIME
1 hour

1. In a heavy saucepan or deep skillet, combine the nopales, half of the onion, the garlic, vinegar, salt, baking powder, and 4 cups water. Cook over medium-high heat, partly covered, for 30 minutes.

2. Drain the nopales using a colander or a large fine-mesh strainer and discard the onion and garlic. Rinse under running cold water for at least a minute. (Note that the nopales exude a slightly slimy liquid that is harmless, but the salad is more appealing if you completely rinse it away.) Let the nopales sit in the colander to drain completely for 10 minutes.

3. Transfer the nopales to a large bowl, along with the remaining onion, the tomatoes, cilantro, chiles and vinegar, pepper, queso fresco, and salt to taste. Serve.

SPAGHETTI WITH POBLANO CHILE SAUCE
(Espagueti Verde)

Espagueti verde is an extremely common dish in Mexican homes. It's so delicious that it ends up being a favorite weeknight dinner (especially when we have roasted and peeled poblano chiles already in the freezer), but its richness makes it especially effective as a first course before a light entrée. Like the Mexican-Style Pasta with Chicken (page 138), this is a proudly Mexican dish, sharing little with Italian cuisine beyond its main ingredient.

1. In a wide saucepan or deep skillet, bring 6 cups water and the salt to a boil over high heat. Add the spaghetti, breaking it in half, if needed, to fit easily into the pan, along with 2 garlic cloves, 1 onion piece, and the oil. Boil for 10 minutes, stirring often, until tender. Strain the pasta over a bowl to keep the cooking liquid and discard the garlic and onion. Rinse the pasta with a little cold running water to stop the cooking and set it aside in the colander or strainer. Wipe the pan clean and set it aside.

2. While the spaghetti cooks, roast the poblanos by placing them directly over a gas flame or under a broiler. Turn them often until their skin is blackened but not disintegrated. Place them in a ziplock bag or covered bowl for at least 5 minutes. When they're cool enough to handle, gently peel and discard the charred skin (it's OK if some remains), then make a lengthwise slit and carefully remove and discard the seeds, veins, and stems.

3. In a blender, combine the poblanos with the remaining garlic clove, the remaining onion piece, the bell pepper, crema, milk, and cream cheese. Blend until very smooth, then pass through a fine-mesh strainer into the pan used to cook the spaghetti.

4. Bring the sauce to a boil over medium-high heat, add the spaghetti, and mix well to distribute the sauce evenly. Add some of the reserved pasta water, if needed, to loosen the sauce. Let the spaghetti heat through for about 1 minute, add salt, if needed, and serve hot.

SERVES 4

1 tablespoon kosher salt

1 pound spaghetti

3 garlic cloves, peeled, divided

½ medium white onion, cut in half

1 tablespoon vegetable oil

2 poblano chiles

1 green bell pepper, stemmed and seeded

1 cup Mexican crema

1 cup whole milk

4 ounces cream cheese

TOTAL COOK TIME

45 minutes

POTATO TAQUITOS
(Flautas de Papa)

This recipe takes me (Reyna) back to my elementary school days. During recess, a woman would stand outside the school with her antojitos (snacks) in a basket and my favorite were the flautas—rolled cigar-shaped crisp-fried tacos sometimes called taquitos dorados—and the potato flauta in particular. She also sold several salsas and my favorite was the salsa macha because of how spicy it was. Sometimes I would even sneak out of school for a few minutes to grab yet another flauta.

Flautas are surprisingly good for large groups or parties. Many people think you have to serve crisp-fried dishes right away and piping hot, but these stay appealingly crunchy-chewy for hours at room temperature.

1. In a large skillet, melt the butter over medium heat. Add the onion and garlic and cook until soft and translucent, 2 to 3 minutes. Add the potatoes, salt, and pepper and fry, stirring occasionally, until the potatoes are soft enough to mash, about 10 minutes. Transfer to a large bowl and mash with a fork or potato masher. Taste and add more salt, if needed. Set aside.

2. Heat the tortillas on a hot comal or griddle, flipping once or twice, until they are soft and pliable, about 30 seconds total (do 2 or 3 at a time if you have a larger griddle). Stack them on a plate as they heat so the residual heat will keep them warm. Stuff each with 2 to 3 tablespoons of the potato mixture, roll, and secure with a toothpick (if you have longer toothpicks, stick them through three flautas at a time).

3. In a large skillet over medium-high heat, pour in oil to a depth of ½ inch. When it starts to shimmer and the edge of a tortilla sizzles on contact, fry the flautas, in batches, if needed, until they are crisp and golden brown, about 2 minutes per side. Drain on paper towels.

4. Serve the flautas hot or warm, garnished with lettuce, crema, queso fresco, and salsa.

SERVES 4

4 tablespoons unsalted butter

¼ small white onion, minced

2 garlic cloves, minced

1 pound yellow, russet, or Yukon Gold potatoes, peeled and diced

¾ teaspoon kosher salt

½ teaspoon freshly ground black pepper

12 store-bought corn tortillas

Vegetable oil, for frying

For serving: shredded iceberg lettuce, Mexican crema, chopped queso fresco, and your choice of salsa

TOTAL COOK TIME

45 minutes

TIPS

Instead of potatoes, flautas can be filled with any sturdy filling you like: shredded chicken, seasoned ground beef, and even grated carrot or mashed cauliflower.

You might want to heat a few extra tortillas in case any break while rolling, but if they're well heated, they should stay pliable.

PAN-FRIED CAULIFLOWER STEAKS
(Milanesa de Coliflor)

Growing up, milanesa was always made with chicken or beef—pounded, breaded, and fried. We'd have it with **Mexican-Style Pasta with Chicken (page 138)** on the side and **Spicy Green Salsa (page 85)** on top. As adults, we thought about making milanesa healthier using a vegetable in place of meat and replacing the traditional corn or vegetable oil with a healthier oil. In many ways, this recipe perfectly reconciles our roots with our present lives. Serve with **Refried Beans (page 49)** and, if desired, **Hibiscus Salsa (page 78)**.

1. Holding the cauliflower stem down, cut in half vertically through the cauliflower core. Working from the middle to the ends, cut "steaks" of ¾-inch thickness (yield will depend on cauliflower size). Reserve the end pieces (that is, any pieces that don't hold together in "steak" form) for another use.

2. In a large saucepan, heat 3½ quarts water and 1½ tablespoons of the salt and bring to a boil over high heat, stirring to dissolve the salt. Add the cauliflower and cook until a butter knife passes easily through the cauliflower cores, about 15 minutes. Using tongs or a slotted spoon, transfer the cauliflower to dry dish towels, working carefully so they don't break. Pat dry and set aside.

3. Prepare your work station: On a large platter or rimmed baking sheet, mix together the breadcrumbs, garlic powder, paprika, pepper, oregano, and the remaining ½ tablespoon salt. In a wide, shallow bowl or rimmed plate, beat the eggs. In two large skillets, big enough to hold at least two cauliflower steaks, add enough avocado oil to each pan to a depth of at least ⅜ inch.

4. Lightly sprinkle flour over both sides of the cauliflower. Coat the cauliflower slices with the egg, letting any excess drip back onto the plate, then coat them evenly with the breadcrumb mixture, pressing so the crumbs adhere.

5. Heat the pans over medium-high heat until the oil shimmers and the edge of a cauliflower floret sizzles on contact. In batches, add the cauliflower and cook until deep golden brown, adjusting the heat, if needed, to avoid burning, 1½ to 2 minutes each side. Transfer to paper towels to drain. Drizzle with 2 tablespoons of the olive oil. Serve right away.

SERVES 4

2 medium cauliflower, leaves removed, stems trimmed

2 tablespoons kosher salt, divided

2¼ cups dried breadcrumbs (we like El Mexicano brand)

2 teaspoons garlic powder

1 teaspoon paprika

1 teaspoon freshly ground black pepper

1 teaspoon dried oregano, crushed to a powder

4 large eggs

Avocado or extra-virgin olive oil, for frying

All-purpose flour, for dusting

2 tablespoons extra-virgin olive oil

TOTAL COOK TIME

45 minutes

6
FROM THE VERACRUZ SEA

"La vida es como la espuma, por eso hay que darse como el mar."

(LIFE IS LIKE SEA FOAM, SO GIVE OF YOURSELF LIKE THE SEA.)

This lovely saying is spoken at a key point in the film *Y Tu Mamá También*. The protagonist is urging her travel companions to be open to everything since life is fleeting. In Veracruz, the sea gives us everything—it's our economy, entertainment, climate, and, of course, key to our diet—so it's a beautiful concept to think of the sea as a symbol of generosity that we should model ourselves after.

SEAFOOD IS QUICK-COOKING AND NUTRITIOUS, perfect for busy weeknight meals. In Veracruz, fishermen wake up at the crack of dawn to fish and sell their catch before dusk. We remember hearing a knock at the door, opening it to find a man holding multiple whole fish hanging from a large wooden rod. Our mother couldn't resist, and she would buy one or two fresh fish for that day's meal.

Unlike meat, which can take an hour or longer to cook and infuse a dish with its flavor, seafood permeates a dish in minutes. One of our most popular tacos is shrimp macha, fresh shrimp sautéed with our salsa macha—a dish that comes together in only three minutes. Any shellfish or fish fillets can be used interchangeably in almost all these dishes.

When I (Reyna) was able to go back to Veracruz after twenty years, I was reminded of how thoroughly seafood is integrated into everyday life. Some of the places I wanted to visit most were the bares botaneros—cantinas famous for their snacks and drinks. In the downtown center near the port is a series of arched colonnades called Los Portales, a festive place filled with live music, but most important, the aroma of fresh seafood. Here, you'll find all the bares botaneros, and they all revolve around seafood: fish tacos, tostadas, ceviches, aguachiles, cocktails, and salads of all kinds of fish and shellfish, including conch and octopus. Of all the botanas (snacks) I had, the albóndigas (meatballs) de pescado at El Chipirón de Los Portales were the most memorable. As a fan of beef meatballs

and, of course, seafood, I wondered why I'd never tried fish albóndigas before. Though El Chipirón has since closed, albóndigas are a common botana at other bars around Los Portales, and I've re-created them here (see page 171).

On the last day of my trip to Veracruz, I was walking through a fish market with my aunt and grandmother. The smell of seafood took me back to my childhood, and it brought back memories of shopping for the perfect fish for our mom to make for dinner. During that walk, we ran into a beloved uncle we call Nan. He offered to make a Fish Salad (page 182) known as minilla—a punchy salad with chipotle, olives, and capers—for my farewell dinner, which was a dish I hadn't had in the twenty years I had been away from home.

We set up a huge table on the patio—aunts, uncles, cousins, and friends all gathered around the table, but more important, around the minilla. We took tostadas and loaded them up with minilla and a creamy green habanero salsa that Nan also made. I'll always remember that afternoon, and how beautiful and delicate my grandmother looked in her woven white shirt. On some level, I think we both knew it would be the last time we shared a meal together. I felt truly at home, as if no time had passed. It was the last I saw of my abuelita before she passed away. I was fortunate enough to have the chance to see her again after so many years, something my siblings were not able to do. I'm so happy to have shared such a deeply joyful afternoon together.

SHRIMP AND SCALLOP AGUACHILE
(Aguachile de Camarón y Callo)

Aguachile is a dish mostly associated with the northern Mexican states along the Gulf of California, like Sinaloa, Sonora, and Baja California. However, it has become increasingly popular in Veracruz, which makes sense since seafood is such a core part of our diet. Best of all, aguachile could not be more healthy or more flavorful. Using large whole shrimp and big meaty sea scallops makes this dish heartier than ceviche made from chopped fish. The avocado provides a creamy contrast to the bracingly tart and spicy sauce (feel free to serve with extra avocado). The recipe multiplies and divides easily, so you can make a giant platter to kick off a celebration, or an outdoor dinner for two on a sunny day with lots of beer.

1. Rinse the scallops and pat dry. If any have the side muscle (a small tough nub) attached, cut it away and discard. Slice each across the middle into two thin discs. Place in a large, wide bowl. Butterfly each shrimp by slicing along its back three-quarters of the way through so it can open like a book, leaving both halves still connected. Press down so they lie flat. Add to the bowl with the scallops and set aside.

2. In a blender, combine the lime juice, lemon juice, cilantro, serranos, salt, and half of the cucumbers and blend until smooth. Add the blended sauce to the bowl with the scallops and shrimp and toss gently so that all the seafood is coated with sauce. Let sit for 15 minutes at room temperature.

3. Slice the remaining cucumbers into thin half-moons and add them to the bowl, along with the red onion; toss gently. Let sit for 5 minutes. Transfer to a platter and garnish with the avocado slices and a drizzle of olive oil. Serve with tostadas.

SERVES 4 TO 8

1 pound sea scallops

1 pound large shrimp, peeled and deveined

¾ cup freshly squeezed lime juice

¾ cup freshly squeezed lemon juice

¾ packed cup fresh cilantro leaves

2 serrano chiles, stemmed

1½ teaspoons kosher salt

1½ cucumbers, peeled, halved lengthwise, and seeded, divided

1 small red onion, very thinly sliced

1 avocado, pitted, peeled, and sliced

extra-virgin olive oil, if desired

16 tostadas

TOTAL COOK TIME

1 hour

FISH MEATBALLS
(Albóndigas de Pescado)

This is our version of the delicious soup served at cantinas in the port of Veracruz, and, honestly, we could eat it daily. The gently spicy tomato broth goes so well with the fish, and its flavor permeates the broth as the fish balls cook. It's a little memory of that first trip back to Veracruz, here in Austin.

1. In a food processor, pulse 6 of the garlic cloves briefly to mince. Add the fish and pulse until finely ground but not yet a paste. Transfer to a large mixing bowl and add the rice, cilantro, egg white, pepper, and $^3/_4$ teaspoon of the salt. Mix with your hands until everything is well combined. Form 16 balls of equal size and set aside, covered.

2. In a large saucepan or Dutch oven, heat 3 tablespoons of the oil over high heat. Add the tomatoes, onion, chiles de árbol, and the remaining 2 garlic cloves and cook for about 3 minutes, or until the onion is translucent and the tomatoes start to break down. Transfer to a blender, along with the remaining $1^1/_4$ teaspoons salt, the oregano, cumin, and 1 cup water. Blend until smooth.

3. In the same pan, heat the remaining 1 tablespoon oil over high heat. Add the zucchini, carrots, and celery and sauté for 2 minutes, stirring occasionally. Add the sauce from the blender, along with 3 cups water (you can first blend the water in the blender to get all the sauce out) and boil for 3 minutes. Taste the broth and add more salt, if needed.

4. Turn the heat down to medium (you want the liquid to be just below a boil) and add the fish balls one at a time. Cook for about 20 minutes, or until the fish is cooked through and the rice is tender (slice into one ball to check). Divide the fish and broth among serving bowls and serve hot with tortillas.

SERVES 4

8 garlic cloves, peeled, divided

1 pound boneless tilapia or red snapper fillets, cut into 2-inch pieces

$^1/_4$ cup long-grain white rice, rinsed and well drained

$^1/_4$ packed cup minced fresh cilantro leaves

1 large egg white

$^1/_4$ teaspoon freshly ground black pepper

2 teaspoons kosher salt, divided

4 tablespoons extra-virgin olive oil, divided

5 Roma tomatoes, quartered

$^1/_2$ medium white onion, cut into 4 pieces

8 chiles de árbol, stemmed and seeded

$^1/_2$ teaspoon dried oregano

$^1/_2$ teaspoon ground cumin

1 large zucchini, cut into 1-inch pieces (about $1^1/_2$ cups)

3 medium carrots, cut into 1-inch pieces (about $1^1/_2$ cups)

1 celery stalk, roughly chopped

Corn Tortillas (page 39) or store-bought, for serving

TOTAL COOK TIME

1 hour

COCONUT RICE WITH SEAFOOD
(Arroz de Coco con Mariscos)

This is our take on the iconic Veracruzano dish called arroz a la tumbada, and the use of coconut milk, which is not typical, is an homage to our love for Thai food. If it were completely up to us, 90 percent of our meals would probably include coconut milk and spicy chiles. This is a great go-to recipe when you're craving seafood because of its versatility. You can use any mix of seafood, or even just all shrimp or all whitefish: Buy whatever is the most fresh and appealing to you. It's a crowd-pleasing one-dish meal, but it also makes a very special side dish or small plate since it pairs well with everything. Spice fans will love this dish with Salsa Macha (page 81).

1. In a large, heavy saucepan or Dutch oven, heat the oil over medium heat. Add the chiles de árbol, garlic, and salt and cook until the garlic starts to brown, about 2 minutes. Add the rice and cook, stirring often, for 3 minutes. Add the coconut milk, onion, red bell pepper, and carrot and cook for 5 minutes; the rice will partly absorb the liquid. Add 4 cups water, stir well, cover, and cook for 5 minutes.

2. Add the shrimp and fish to the pot; cover, turn the heat down to low, and simmer for about 15 minutes, or until the rice and seafood are both cooked through. Toss gently, then garnish with the cilantro and serve.

SERVES 4 TO 6

2 tablespoons extra-virgin olive oil

10 chiles de árbol, stemmed

10 garlic cloves, minced

2 teaspoons kosher salt

2 cups long-grain white rice, rinsed and well drained

1 (14-ounce) can unsweetened coconut milk

1 medium red onion, cut into large dice

1 large red bell pepper, stemmed, seeded, and cut into large dice

1 carrot, peeled and sliced into ½-inch rounds

1 pound jumbo shrimp, peeled and deveined

8 ounces boneless steelhead trout fillets, cut into 1-inch pieces (or substitute salmon, arctic char, or tuna)

8 ounces boneless tilapia fillets, cut into 1-inch pieces (or substitute any white fish)

¼ cup chopped fresh cilantro leaves

TOTAL COOK TIME

1 hour

GARLIC-CHIPOTLE SHRIMP
(Camarones al Mojo de Ajo Enchipotlados)

Shrimp are one of the most common proteins in Veracruz. Most markets have all kinds of locally caught shrimp in rainbow colors—white, pink, red, brown—in sizes ranging from inch-long rock shrimp (with a texture and flavor like lobster) to king shrimp that can reach nine inches or more. In dishes like this where shrimp is the star, buy whichever variety is the freshest and most flavorful. This dish combines both garlic shrimp and chipotle shrimp into one. Either would be great on its own—the very garlicky shrimp without the salsa, or shrimp seared in the chipotle salsa without the garlic marinade—but together, they're heaven. If I (Reyna) had to pick one favorite recipe in this book, it would be this one.

1. To make the salsa, in a small saucepan, bring 1 cup of water and the moritas to a boil over high heat. Reduce the heat to medium-low, cover, and cook for 15 minutes. Add the tomatoes and cook for an additional 5 minutes, stirring occasionally to avoid sticking, if needed. Transfer to a blender with the garlic and salt and puree until very smooth.

2. In a large skillet, heat the oil over medium heat. Add the blender contents (careful, it will splatter) and cook for about 3 minutes, or until the sauce is thick but not quite a paste (add a little water, if needed). Taste and add salt, if needed. Set aside.

3. To make the shrimp, in a blender or food processor, grind the garlic, salt, white vinegar, and pepper with 2 tablespoons water until it becomes a paste. Coat the shrimp with the mixture and let it sit at room temperature for 5 to 10 minutes.

4. In a very large skillet (large enough to hold all the shrimp in a single layer), heat the oil and the butter over medium-high heat. When the oil and butter are sizzling hot, add the shrimp. Cook just until cooked through, 2 to 3 minutes per side.

5. To serve, you can stir in the salsa to coat the shrimp, place the shrimp on top of the salsa on a serving platter, or offer the salsa in a separate bowl at the table.

SERVES 4

FOR THE SALSA:

10 morita or other chipotle chiles, stemmed and seeded

5 Roma tomatoes, quartered

5 garlic cloves, peeled

1½ teaspoons kosher salt

2 tablespoons vegetable oil

FOR THE SHRIMP:

20 garlic cloves, peeled

2 teaspoons kosher salt

1 teaspoon white or cider vinegar

1 teaspoon freshly ground black pepper

2½ pounds head-on, unpeeled jumbo shrimp, or 1½ pounds headless, peeled jumbo shrimp

2 tablespoons vegetable oil

2 tablespoons unsalted butter

TOTAL COOK TIME

45 minutes

TIP

This is one case where we don't recommend using canned chipotles, as they make the sauce too sweet.

SHRIMP CEVICHE
(Ceviche de Camarón)

Ceviche is super common in any marisquería (seafood restaurant) in Veracruz. When we opened our brick-and-mortar restaurant, Veracruz Fonda & Bar, we knew we needed to make ceviche a permanent appetizer, served with salsa and totopos (chips) to enjoy on a hot day since it's light and fresh. It's become such a favorite that nearly every table orders it. Key to this dish is waiting until the last minute to mix the vegetables in with the shrimp.

1. Cut the shrimp crosswise into 4 pieces (freezing them for 20 to 30 minutes can make the cutting easier). Rinse the shrimp under cold water, drain well, pat dry, and place them in a nonreactive bowl. Add the lime juice, mix well, cover, and refrigerate for at least 4 hours and up to 12 hours.

2. While the shrimp marinates, in a separate bowl, combine the red bell pepper, onion, cilantro, garlic, serrano, salt, onion powder, and black pepper, then cover and refrigerate.

3. When ready to serve, drain most of the liquid from the shrimp and stir in the vegetable mixture. Taste and add more salt, if needed.

SERVES 4

1 pound large shrimp, peeled and deveined

2 cups freshly squeezed lime juice (about 15 limes)

½ red bell pepper, seeded and diced

½ small red onion, minced

¼ packed cup fresh cilantro leaves, chopped

1 garlic clove, minced

1 serrano chile, stemmed and minced

½ teaspoon kosher salt

¼ teaspoon onion powder

¼ teaspoon freshly ground black pepper

Tostadas or tortilla chips, for serving

TOTAL COOK TIME

30 minutes, plus 4 hours marinating time

COLD TUNA-STUFFED JALAPEÑO CHILES

(Chiles Rellenos en Frío)

Because they are finger food and served at room temperature, chiles en frío are the perfect party food, and for some reason they're especially popular around Christmas. This canned-tuna filling is traditional and delicious, but you could also stuff them with Fish Salad (page 182). Quick-cooking the chiles in the vinegar-spiked bath helps mitigate their heat, as does removing the veins and seeds (save the veins to make Jalapeño-Egg Fritter, page 104).

1. To prepare the chiles, make a slice down one side of each jalapeño and remove the veins and seeds while keeping the whole chile intact. Fill a medium pot with 6 cups water and bring the pot to a boil over high heat. Once boiling, add the chiles, vinegar, sugar, salt, garlic, bay leaves, fresh thyme, and the oregano and cook for 5 minutes. Drain well, reserving 1 cup of the cooking liquid, and set the chiles aside.

2. To make the tuna filling, in a small bowl, combine the tuna, mayonnaise, and crema. Season with salt and pepper to taste. Using a small spoon, stuff the chiles with the tuna filling and place them on a platter.

3. To make the carrots and onion mixture, in a small saucepan, heat the reserved chile water over medium heat and add the carrots. Cover and cook until they are tender, about 8 minutes. Drain the carrots and let them cool.

4. In a medium skillet, heat the oil over high heat and add the onion. Once it starts to turn transparent, add the oregano, vinegar, and salt, along with the cooked carrots. Cook, stirring often, for 3 minutes.

5. Serve the chiles at room temperature with the onion-carrot mixture strewn over the top. Alternatively, the components can all be prepared separately and stored in the refrigerator, to be assembled before serving.

SERVES 2 TO 4

FOR THE CHILES:

10 jalapeño chiles, stemmed

⅓ cup white vinegar

1 tablespoon sugar

1 tablespoon kosher salt

2 large garlic cloves, peeled

4 dried bay leaves

1 tablespoon fresh or dried thyme

1 tablespoon dried oregano

FOR THE TUNA FILLING:

1 (8-ounce) can tuna, drained

⅓ cup mayonnaise

3 tablespoons Mexican crema

Kosher salt and freshly ground black pepper

FOR THE CARROTS AND ONION:

2 medium carrots, peeled and sliced ⅛ inch thick (about 1 cup)

¼ cup extra-virgin olive oil

1 medium white onion, thinly sliced

½ teaspoon dried oregano

1 tablespoon apple cider vinegar

¼ teaspoon kosher salt

TOTAL COOK TIME

1 hour

VERACRUZ-STYLE SNAPPER
(Huachinango a la Veracruzana)

This is one of the most iconic dishes in Veracruz, with the capers, olives, and wine highlighting the Spanish influence on the cuisine. It's often served with white rice and potatoes, but we prefer this more stew-like and less starchy version.

When we were younger, our mom would make this dish using a whole fish, wrapping everything in foil and cooking it over a fire. Maritza, though, didn't like eating whole fish, so our dad would always tuck in a boneless fillet for her. When we started re-creating this dish as adults, we found that cooking boneless fillets in a pan was our favorite version. This way, we could make it with a higher ratio of sauce to fish to soak up at the table with crusty Mexican rolls called bolillos.

1. Pat the fish fillets dry. In a small dish, mix 2 teaspoons of the salt with the garlic powder and pepper. Sprinkle the seasoning evenly on both sides of the fish.

2. Heat a large cast-iron skillet over high heat for 3 minutes. Drizzle in 2 tablespoons of the oil and immediately add the fish, skin side down, in a single layer. Cook undisturbed for 1 minute, then flip and sear the other side for 30 seconds. Transfer to a plate (it's OK if some fish bits remain in the pan).

3. Turn the heat down to medium, adding the remaining 1 tablespoon oil, the remaining 1 teaspoon salt, and the onion. Cook for about 30 seconds, or until the onion starts to turn translucent, then add the garlic, jalapeño, and red bell peppers. Cook for about 2 minutes, or until the peppers start to lightly brown. Add the wine, scraping up any browned bits, then add the tomatoes. Turn the heat up to high and cook for about 3 minutes, or until the tomatoes break down.

4. Add the broth, bay leaves, thyme, capers, olives, and 1 cup water and bring to a boil. Boil for 3 minutes, adding additional broth if the mixture gets too dry (it should be a thick, stew-like consistency). Turn the heat down to medium-low and place the fish, skin side up, on top of the sauce, then arrange the lemon slices on top of the fish.

5. Cook for about 4 minutes, or just until the fish is cooked through, then serve from the pan or carefully transfer to a platter. Garnish with the parsley and serve immediately.

SERVES 4

4 (6-ounce) skin-on red snapper fillets

3 teaspoons kosher salt, divided

1 teaspoon garlic powder

½ teaspoon freshly ground black pepper

3 tablespoons extra-virgin olive oil, divided

½ cup thinly sliced white onion

10 garlic cloves, thinly sliced

1 jalapeño chile, stemmed, seeded, and cut into thin strips

1 red bell pepper, stemmed, seeded, and julienned

1 green bell pepper, stemmed, seeded, and julienned

½ cup dry white wine

1 pound Roma tomatoes, cut into 1-inch pieces (about 2 cups)

½ cup Seafood Broth (page 56), or store-bought, plus more as needed

4 dried bay leaves

6 fresh thyme sprigs, leaves chopped

2 teaspoons capers

16 pitted black olives (such as kalamata)

1 lemon, sliced into 8 rounds and seeded

¼ cup chopped fresh parsley

TOTAL COOK TIME

45 minutes

TIP

A baguette or other crusty French rolls can be used in place of bolillos, and corn tortillas are a gluten-free option.

FISH SALAD
(Minilla de Pescado)

This dish is ubiquitous in Veracruz, and makes a delicious and healthy lunch or topping for tostadas. With powerful flavors like chipotle, olive, caper, garlic, and wine, it's far more complex than a typical tuna salad (which it sometimes gets compared to in the US), but it remains light and never obscures the flavor and texture of the fresh fish. It used to be most commonly made with small sharks—our grandmother would always say, "Para hacer minilla necesitas cazón" (To make minilla, you need shark)—but we use other fish with a similar dense and meaty texture, like halibut, cobia, sturgeon, or mahi-mahi. Some Veracruzanos make this dish with tuna, which is also an option if you're a tuna fan. Minilla also makes a nice empanada filling, pickled jalapeño chile stuffing, or accompaniment to White Rice (page 46).

1. To make the fish, fill a medium saucepan halfway with water and add the fish, salt, garlic, onion, and herbs (if using), stirring gently to partially dissolve the salt (it will fully dissolve as it heats). Bring to a boil over high heat. Cook at a boil for at least 10 minutes, or until the fish breaks apart easily with a fork (be careful not to overcook). Using a slotted spoon or tongs, carefully transfer the fish to a plate, discard the onion and garlic, and shred coarsely using two forks. Set aside.

2. To make the minilla, in a large skillet, heat the oil over high heat. Add the onion, tomatoes, garlic, chipotles, and adobo, olives, capers, and salt. Cook until the onion softens, 3 to 5 minutes. Add the wine and cook, stirring often, until most of the wine has reduced; the mixture should be very moist but not watery. Remove the pan from the heat and gently stir in the shredded fish. Serve at room temperature or refrigerate until needed, bringing the dish to room temperature before serving with tostadas or totopos.

SERVES 4 TO 8

FOR THE FISH:

2 pounds boneless and skinless fish steaks or fillets, such as halibut, cobia, sturgeon, or mahi-mahi

2 teaspoons kosher salt

4 garlic cloves, halved

½ medium white onion, roughly chopped

Mix of fresh sage, rosemary, thyme, oregano, bay leaf (optional)

TO FINISH THE MINILLA:

3 tablespoons extra-virgin olive oil

½ medium white onion, diced

7 Roma tomatoes, diced

6 garlic cloves, minced

2 canned chipotle chiles in adobo, minced, plus 1 teaspoon adobo from the can

12 pitted black olives (such as kalamata), minced

2 teaspoons capers, chopped if large

1 teaspoon kosher salt

2 cups dry white wine

Homemade or good-quality tostadas or totopos (chips), for serving

TOTAL COOK TIME

45 minutes

GRILLED WHOLE POMPANO
(Pompano Asado)

We grew up eating all kinds of fish in Veracruz, and after being gone for many years, we started to forget which fish corresponded to which dish. We tried to re-create each one to the best of our abilities, but the snapper and sea bass in Austin grocery stores didn't much resemble the huachinango or lubina of our youth.

One day I (Reyna) saw "pompano" at the farmers market in Mueller Park, and since the name was familiar (we call it pámpano), I decided to try it, and I was immediately brought back to Veracruz. There, it's sometimes called "pez mantequilla"—butterfish—for its rich but delicate flavor and texture. Ever since then, it's been my go-to for whole fish grilling. You can substitute snapper, sole, or grouper if you can't find pompano. Grilling in my house happens at least twice a week for dinner, and a fish is involved at least once. This recipe is perfect for a group, since it's just as easy to grill several fish as it is to grill just one.

SERVES 4 TO 6

3 (1½-pound) whole pompanos (or 1 or 2 larger fish to total 4 to 5 pounds), cleaned, head and tail intact

6 garlic cloves, peeled

1 tablespoon kosher salt

1 teaspoon freshly ground black pepper

2 lemons, juiced, lemon halves reserved

2 tablespoons extra-virgin olive oil, plus more for brushing

Mango salsa (see page 186), with or without the mango, for serving

Salsa Macha (page 81), for serving

Corn Tortillas (page 39) or store-bought, or flour tortillas, for serving

TOTAL COOK TIME
30 minutes, plus 1½ hours marinating time

1. Rinse the fish and pat dry. Slash 2 or 3 cuts through the skin on both sides of each fish. Place the fish on a rimmed baking sheet.

2. Mince the garlic, salt, and pepper until it becomes a paste. Transfer to a small bowl and mix in the lemon juice (reserving the lemon halves) and oil. Coat the fish evenly—inside and out—with this mixture. Place the spent lemon halves in the bellies of the fish, slicing them in half if they are too bulky. Cover the fish with plastic wrap and refrigerate for at least 1 hour and up to 24 hours. Remove from the refrigerator 30 minutes before cooking.

3. Preheat the grill to 400°F to 500°F. (If your grill doesn't have a thermometer, use the hand test: Hold your hand 5 inches above the grill grates; when you have to pull your hand away after 3 to 4 seconds, you're in the right heat range.) Oil the grill. Brush one side of each fish generously with oil and place, oiled side down, on the grill. Cook without moving for about 5 minutes, or until the skin is dark and crisp but not burned. Brush the top of the fish with oil and flip the fish. Cook for another 5 minutes; the fish is done when it flakes easily with a fork or reaches an internal temperature of 145°F (on an instant-read thermometer). Cooking time will vary with the size of fish.

4. Serve hot, with the mango salsa on top and with salsa macha and tortillas alongside.

FISH TACOS WITH MANGO SALSA
(Tacos de Pescado con Salsa de Mango)

When we moved to Austin, most of the fish taco places offered Baja-style tacos, battered and deep-fried. They can be excellent, but they're not something we like to eat regularly. When creating the menu for Veracruz All Natural, we wanted to include a healthy fish taco that would fit more diets. This fish taco is light and fresh, and the more salsa you add, the better it tastes. Something about the sweet and sour of the mango and lime balanced against the creamy cheese gives this recipe the perfect flavor combination.

1. To make the salsa, in a medium bowl, combine the tomatoes, mangoes, onion, cilantro, lime juice, and salt and stir well. Taste and adjust any ingredients to taste, then set aside.

2. To make the tacos, lightly salt the fish on both sides. In a large skillet (preferably nonstick), heat the oil over medium heat. Working in batches if necessary, add the fillets in a single layer and cook for about 4 minutes each side, or just until cooked through. The fish should flake easily with a fork. Transfer each fillet to a plate once cooked. Add more oil as needed if cooking in batches.

3. While the fish cooks, heat the tortillas on a large comal or griddle. Divide the cheese among the tortillas and heat until the cheese has melted. You can also make a "costra" by flipping each one, cheese-side down, on the comal until the cheese turns brown and starts to crisp, at which point it will slightly pull away from the comal and allow you to flip it back cheese-side up.

4. Assemble each taco on a tortilla with fish, cabbage, mango salsa, avocado, and the jalapeño salsa, if using.

SERVES 4

FOR THE MANGO SALSA:

3 Roma tomatoes, minced, juices reserved

2 mangoes, peeled, pitted, and minced

1 small red onion, minced

¾ packed cup fresh cilantro leaves, minced

2 tablespoons freshly squeezed lime juice

1½ teaspoons kosher salt

FOR THE TACOS:

Kosher salt

2 pounds boneless tilapia fillets, cut into 8 roughly equal pieces (or substitute another firm white fish, like snapper)

¼ cup vegetable oil, plus more as needed

8 Corn Tortillas (page 39) or store-bought, or flour tortillas

8 ounces Monterey Jack, mozzarella, or cheddar cheese, grated

¼ head green cabbage, shredded

1 avocado, pitted, peeled, and cut into 8 slices

Creamy Jalapeño Salsa (page 73), optional

TOTAL COOK TIME
45 minutes

SHRIMP IN SPICY CREAM SAUCE
(Camarones Enchilpayados)

Camarones enchilpayados, made from juicy, never frozen, head-on shrimp, was the first thing my aunt served me (Reyna) when we reunited, and it was one of the last dishes I shared with my grandmother before she passed away. I was determined to replicate it when I came home, and managed to develop a version, using piquín chiles from my garden, that reminds me of our extended family every time I make it.

Depending on who you ask, chilpaya chiles are either a close relative to, or just the Veracruzano name for, the dried chile known elsewhere as piquín, chiltepín, and amashito. It's small and hot, but here it becomes manageable when tempered with the mayo, yogurt, and crema (Maritza's daughter, Lis, has a low-heat threshold but loves this dish). Piquín chiles are easy to find, but you could substitute chiles de árbol in a pinch—the flavor will be different but still delicious. We prefer to use head-on shrimp because the heads contribute flavor, but cleaned headless shrimp will work well, too. The mayonnaise adds terrific flavor and texture here, but anyone who doesn't eat eggs or otherwise dislikes mayonnaise can substitute canned unsweetened coconut milk and reduce the water to a half cup.

1. In a large bowl, place the shrimp. In a blender, grind the garlic, peppercorns, salt, and 1/4 cup water until it becomes a paste. Coat the shrimp with the paste and let it sit at room temperature for 20 to 30 minutes.

2. In a small skillet, cook the chilpayas over medium heat, stirring often, until they start to change color and smell toasty, but not burned, about 1 minute. Transfer them to a blender, along with the mayonnaise, yogurt, crema, and 1 cup water and blend until smooth. Set aside.

3. In a very large skillet (large enough to hold all the shrimp in a single layer), heat the butter and oil over medium-high heat. When the pan is sizzling hot, add the shrimp. Cook for 2 to 3 minutes, until they are golden brown on one side. Flip the shrimp, add the red onion, and cook without moving for 2 minutes. Add the blender mixture, stir well, and bring to a boil. Add salt, if needed, and serve immediately with rice or tortillas.

SERVES 4

2½ pounds head-on, unpeeled jumbo shrimp, or 1½ pounds headless, peeled jumbo shrimp

12 garlic cloves, peeled

1 teaspoon black peppercorns

1 teaspoon kosher salt

2 tablespoons chilpaya or piquín chiles

½ cup mayonnaise

½ cup Greek yogurt (not low-fat)

½ cup Mexican crema

2 tablespoons unsalted butter

1 tablespoon extra-virgin olive oil

1 medium red onion, thinly sliced (about 2 cups)

White Rice (page 46) or Corn Tortillas (page 39) or store-bought, for serving

TOTAL COOK TIME

1 hour

7
MEAT AND POULTRY

"Hay que echar toda la carne al asador."

(YOU HAVE TO THROW ALL THE MEAT ON THE GRILL.)

In other words, you have to go all in for your dreams to become real.

I (Maritza) came to the United States in 1999 right after the rest of the family. To make ends meet, I took a job as a waitress in the same restaurant where Reyna was already working as a server. I worked nights for a while, and I struggled with the language; sometimes I felt humiliated in front of customers. However, these painful moments made me even more determined to succeed. I took on accounting and administrative responsibilities, learning skills that I eventually used in our businesses.

YEARS LATER, I ULTIMATELY MADE the difficult decision to separate from my first husband while supporting a ten-year-old and a toddler. Luckily, I had a mother who was both forceful and resilient, and with her example, I knew I wanted to do more for my kids to set them up for a future with better opportunities than I had. Making the decision to partner with Reyna and start our own restaurant was not hard. I believed so much in her and in our vision. Still, as a single mother of two kids, there was a lot of uncertainty and fear at this point in my journey.

Throughout the process, there were times where we couldn't pay our utility bills, and days where we questioned whether we were going to be able to have a full meal. When the electricity was cut off, I would pretend that the candles we used to light our house were part of an adventure, so the kids wouldn't see how hard our situation was. In the scorching Texas heat, my son would sit outside after school or on weekends, and I would place a battery-operated fan in front of him. At one point, I bought him a small kiddie pool that I placed in a shady spot behind the food truck to keep him cool. We constantly missed out on activities from school and other things kids his age should be doing, but knowing that the sacrifices and hardships would lead to something that would impact generations to come kept us going.

Most of the recipes in this chapter are inspired by the frugality of those early years, turning a little meat and some inexpensive pantry items into indulgent meals like Beef and Cactus Paddles (page 197) and Veracruzano Chicken Stew (page 209). As much as we like to follow healthy diets, we both eat (responsibly raised) meat and see it as neither a necessity nor a luxury, just one of many wonderful sources of protein. For us, however, the sauce and technique in these dishes are generally more important than the meat itself. Because of that, all these recipes lend themselves to vegetarian substitutes like sturdy vegetables, mushrooms, greens, tofu, beans, lentils, or queso fresco. You can also substitute the meat of your choice, such as chicken for steak.

These dishes (except the fried chicken) can be made ahead and reheated, making it easy to repurpose leftovers as fillings for tacos or Picadas (page 42). While these are main dishes, quantities can be reduced to serve as appetizers before a main dish of vegetables or seafood, to flip the "meat as main course" narrative.

MEATBALLS IN CHIPOTLE BROTH
(Albóndigas en Chipotle)

This is comfort food in a bowl. We prefer a soupier version (some albóndigas en chipotle feature meatballs coated in a thick sauce) so there's more tasty broth to soak up with the white rice we serve with this. Most recipes advise to brown the meatballs in oil first, but we cook them in the sauce, which is easier and healthier, and allows the meat to soak up tons of flavor from the broth.

　　Waxy potatoes, such as red or new potatoes, hold up well in soups, keeping their shape. Higher-starch potatoes, like russets, tend to fall apart—which some people like, because it thickens the soup with an almost creamy texture. We think Yukon Golds are the best of both worlds: Here, they hold their shape when cooking and serving but fall apart when you nudge them with your spoon.

1. To make the meatballs, mince the garlic, salt, and pepper until it becomes a paste, and transfer it to a large bowl. Add the meat and egg and mix everything together well until all the ingredients are fully combined. Form about 20 golf ball–size meatballs and chill on a plate in the refrigerator until needed.

2. To make the soup, in a blender, combine the tomatoes, onion, and chipotles and blend until smooth. In a medium saucepan or stockpot, heat the oil over high heat. Add the blended tomato mixture (careful, it will splatter) and cook for about 15 seconds, then add the salt, bay leaves, and 2 cups water. Bring to a boil and cook for 3 minutes, then turn the heat down to medium and add the potatoes and meatballs. Cook at a low boil—you don't want the meatballs to fall apart—until the meat is cooked through and the potatoes are very soft, about 15 minutes. Taste and add more salt and/or adobo from the chipotle can. Serve in large shallow bowls over rice.

SERVES 4

FOR THE MEATBALLS:

3 garlic cloves, peeled

2 teaspoons kosher salt

1½ teaspoons freshly ground black pepper

2 pounds ground beef, pork, or a mix

1 large egg

TO FINISH THE SOUP:

1½ pounds Roma tomatoes, quartered

½ small white onion, chopped

5 whole canned chipotle chiles in adobo

¼ cup vegetable oil

1¼ teaspoons kosher salt

2 dried bay leaves

1 pound Yukon Gold potatoes, peeled and cut into 1-inch pieces

White Rice (page 46), for serving

TOTAL COOK TIME

45 minutes

BEEF AND CACTUS PADDLES
(Bistec con Nopales)

Nopales, aka cactus paddles (as well as cruzetas, which are cousins to nopales), have always been a key part of our diet. They grow wild and abundant in Veracruz, so they are both economical and ultra-fresh. We grew up eating them on their own, with eggs and beans, and in soups and salads, but having them with steak was always a favorite, as it marked special occasions. Learning how to pick and clean nopales was something of a rite of passage—it takes patience and time, something always worth teaching kids. Getting pricked by the tiny thorns was an omnipresent risk, since many are impossible to see. But it has proved to be a valuable skill, as it means that we can always buy the freshest nopales, since they degenerate quickly in quality once cut. Serve with tortillas, salsa, and rice and/or beans.

1. Pound the steak to a thickness of about ¼ inch, using a mallet or anything heavy, like a rolling pin or the bottom of a cast-iron skillet. Your result should be an evenly shaped rectangle. With the long side facing you, roll the steak up (like a jelly roll) and cut into slices about ¾ inch thick. In a large bowl, add the steak, garlic, cilantro, Jamaica seasoning, salt, and 1 tablespoon of the oil. Mix well with your hands, cover, and refrigerate for at least 1 hour and up to 12 hours.

2. In a large heavy skillet (preferably cast iron), heat the remaining 1 tablespoon oil over high heat. When very hot, add the meat and cook for 3 minutes, stirring almost continuously. Add the nopales, onion, and serrano and keep stirring for another 5 minutes. At this point, the onions and nopales should be softened. Serve at this stage, or cook longer if you prefer more well-cooked meat. Top with the queso fresco before serving.

SERVES 4

1 pound skirt steak or flank steak

4 garlic cloves, minced

¼ packed cup fresh cilantro leaves, minced

2 teaspoons flor de Jamaica (dried hibiscus flowers (see page 206)

¾ teaspoon kosher salt

2 tablespoons extra-virgin olive oil, divided

4 ounces cleaned fresh nopales (cactus paddles), cut into ½-inch strips (about 1¼ cups sliced)

¼ medium white onion, thinly sliced

1 serrano chile, stemmed and thinly sliced

¼ cup crumbled queso fresco

TOTAL COOK TIME

30 minutes, plus 1 hour marinating time

TIPS

Skirt and flank steak both work well here. Skirt steak is a little thinner and fattier, and flank, though thicker and tougher, is tenderized by the pounding process. Otherwise, the cooking time and flavor will be similar.

Fresh nopales—whether with thorns, dethorned, or already sliced or chopped—are readily available in most Mexican markets.

STEAK AND ONIONS
(Bistec Encebollado)

Beef and onions become a luxurious dish when using tenderloin steak (from which the filet mignon is cut). On the rare occasions that we ate beef as kids, it was either a la mexicana (with tomatoes and chiles) or this way, smothered in onions. Serving this with White Rice (page 46), Black or Refried Beans (page 49), and Corn Tortillas (page 39) makes for a simple meal packed with so much flavor.

1. Mince the garlic, salt, and pepper until it becomes a paste. In a large bowl, coat the beef well with the garlic paste, and let it sit for at least 5 minutes.

2. In a large, deep skillet, heat the oil over high heat. Add the beef and cook until it is deeply browned, about 2 minutes per side. Add the onion and serranos (if using) and cook, stirring often, for about 5 minutes, or until the onions are soft and sweet and the beef has reached an internal temperature of 130°F at its thickest point. Remove the steak from the pan and let it sit for 5 to 10 minutes before slicing.

3. While the steak rests, make sure the onions are fully cooked, then deglaze the pan with 2 tablespoons water, scraping up all the browned bits to mix with the onion. Slice the steak and serve smothered in the onions.

SERVES 4

2 garlic cloves, peeled

1 teaspoon kosher salt

1 teaspoon freshly ground black pepper

1 pound beef tenderloin

¼ cup vegetable oil

1 large white onion (about 1 pound), very thinly sliced

1 to 2 serrano chiles, stemmed and thinly sliced (optional)

TOTAL COOK TIME

30 minutes

PORK CARNITAS
(Carnitas de Cerdo)

Our uncles used to kill whole pigs to make carnitas for quinceañeras or weddings. The basic process of making carnitas—letting the pork braise in its fat—is very simple, but given the complexity of our uncles' version, we knew they must be harboring flavor secrets that we were determined to know. We asked our nephew, who grew up making carnitas, for some pointers, and with his suggestions, we spent months trying to perfect this dish. The result, we're proud to say, is even better than what we remember as kids.

Carnitas can be served myriad ways—even just on its own with beans or tortillas—but we serve it with fresh hot tortillas, salsa, lime wedges, minced white onion, minced cilantro, diced avocado or guacamole, and beans and/or rice.

Carnitas freezes well. Pack the meat with a little of the lard that's left in the pot after cooking into ziplock bags and pat them flat (for quicker thawing); the thawed meat can be reheated over medium heat for 5 minutes, or until hot throughout.

1. To make the marinade for the pork, mince the garlic, salt, and pepper until it becomes a paste. In a large bowl, coat the pork evenly with the mixture, cover, and refrigerate for at least 8 hours and up to 2 days.

2. When ready to cook, in a blender, combine the orange juice, evaporated milk, beer, lime juice, Coke, onion, garlic, vinegar, thyme, oregano, salt, and allspice and blend until smooth. Set aside.

3. In a large Dutch oven, heat the lard over medium-high heat until it starts to bubble; the temperature should be between 250°F and 275°F. Add the pork carefully to minimize splatter. Cook for 20 minutes, turning the pork pieces occasionally so they don't stick.

4. Turn the heat down to medium-low and cook for 1 minute more, then add the blended mixture along with the reserved orange halves, bay leaves, and chiles de árbol. Check the temperature of the mixture: You want to maintain it between 200°F and 225°F for the rest of the cooking process. Cook, turning the pork occasionally to avoid sticking, for at least 1½ hours, or until the meat is soft enough to be pulled apart by tongs or forks. By the end of cooking, the meat should be a rich dark color on the outside and very tender on the inside. Discard the bay leaves. Pull the meat apart and serve.

SERVES 8 TO 12

FOR THE PORK:

8 garlic cloves, peeled

1½ tablespoons kosher salt

1 teaspoon freshly ground black pepper

4 pounds boneless pork roast (Boston butt), cut into 4 pieces

TO FINISH:

2 oranges, halved and juiced (about ½ cup juice), halves reserved

⅔ cup evaporated milk

½ cup beer (preferably amber or IPA)

⅓ cup freshly squeezed lime juice

¼ cup Coca-Cola (preferably Mexican Coke)

½ medium white onion

5 garlic cloves, peeled

1 tablespoon apple cider vinegar

1 teaspoon dried thyme

1 teaspoon dried oregano

1 teaspoon kosher salt

¼ teaspoon ground allspice

4 cups pork lard

5 dried bay leaves

5 chiles de árbol, stemmed

TOTAL COOK TIME

2½ hours, plus 8 hours marinating time

TIP

Strain the leftover lard and use it to fry refried beans, to sear shrimp, or to cook thin-cut meat for tacos. It keeps for at least 2 weeks in the refrigerator.

CHILE-ROASTED PORK
(Puerco en Adobo)

Along with Cold Tuna-Stuffed Jalapeño Chiles (page 178), this is a dish that we associate with Christmas. It's a great example of how a relatively inexpensive cut of meat can become an impressive holiday centerpiece when combined with the deep complexity of dried chiles. Ask your butcher to cut the pork into pieces so that the marinade and salsa can deeply infuse the meat. It also helps it fit into a roasting pan, but by all means, you can keep it in one piece and just break it up at the table if you wish.

1. To make the marinade for the pork, in a blender, combine the garlic, salt, vinegar, peppercorns, and 6 tablespoons water and blend to a paste (add more water, if needed, to keep the blades turning). Rinse the meat well, pat it dry, and place into a large bowl. Add the marinade, toss to coat, and set aside for 30 minutes while you make the adobo sauce. Reserve the blender for the adobo sauce (no need to rinse it). Heat the oven to 350°F.

2. To make the adobo sauce, in a medium saucepan, bring 2 cups water to a boil and add the moritas. Boil for about 5 minutes, or until the chiles are soft. Meanwhile, in a large skillet, heat the oil over medium-high heat. Add the pasillas and anchos and cook, turning them often, until they become fragrant and start to blister, about 1 minute. (Be careful not to let them burn.) Add the chiles to the saucepan with the moritas, turn off the heat, and let soak for 10 minutes.

3. Add the chiles to the blender with 1 cup of the soaking liquid, the salt, cloves, and cumin seeds. Blend until very smooth, about 2 minutes, to fully break down the chile skins.

4. Using your hands, spread the butter evenly over the pork, then coat the pork with the adobo sauce from the blender (you can use a wooden spoon or other implement here so the chiles don't stain your hands). Place the pork in a roasting pan, cover tightly with aluminum foil, and bake for 2 hours. Check it at this point and cook longer if necessary, until the meat easily pulls apart with a fork. Serve the pork on a platter with all the juices, plus hot tortillas, rice, and beans.

SERVES 6 TO 10

FOR THE PORK:

10 garlic cloves, peeled

2 tablespoons kosher salt

1½ tablespoons apple cider vinegar

1½ teaspoons black peppercorns

6 pounds bone-in pork shoulder (Boston butt), cut into 4 pieces by your butcher

FOR THE ADOBO SAUCE:

2 morita chiles, stemmed and seeded

2 tablespoons vegetable oil

2 pasilla chiles, stemmed and seeded

8 ancho chiles, stemmed and seeded

1 teaspoon kosher salt

5 whole cloves

1½ teaspoons whole cumin seeds

2 tablespoons unsalted butter, at room temperature

Corn Tortillas (page 39) or store-bought, White Rice (page 46), and Refried Beans (page 49), for serving

TOTAL COOK TIME

3 hours

ACHIOTE AND CITRUS-BRAISED PORK
(Cochinita Pibil)

Though the port of Veracruz is a twelve-hour drive from the state of Yucatán, we share the Gulf of Mexico and a reverence for each other's cuisines. Cochinita pibil is perhaps the best-known and ubiquitous dish from Yucatán, but it's also common in taquerías and home kitchens along the length of Veracruz. Achiote, too, is an ingredient closely connected with Yucatán, but it's grown widely in Veracruz and used to add color and flavor to fish, seafood dishes, and tamales, as well as chicken (see Achiote Chicken, page 218). Serve this pork with red onions pickled with lime and habanero, in tacos, and/or with White Rice (page 46) or Mexican Rice (page 47).

1. In a blender, combine the garlic, salt, peppercorns, vinegar, and 2 tablespoons water and blend until smooth. In a large bowl, combine the pork and blended mixture and let it sit for up to 1 hour at room temperature, or cover and refrigerate for up to 24 hours.

2. While the pork marinates, add the orange juice, lime juice, achiote, oregano, and 2 cups water to the blender (no need to rinse blender) and blend until smooth. Set aside until ready to cook, or cover and refrigerate along with the pork.

3. In a large Dutch oven or stockpot, heat the oil over high heat and sear the pork (reserving the marinade), turning it often, until it is dark brown on all sides, about 10 minutes total. Add the reserved marinade, juice mixture, and 6 cups water and bring to a boil. Turn the heat down to a simmer, cover, and cook for at least 1¹/₂ hours, or until the meat is easily pulled from the bone with a fork or tongs. Serve.

SERVES 4 TO 8

12 garlic cloves, peeled

1½ tablespoons kosher salt

1½ teaspoons black peppercorns

1 teaspoon white vinegar

4 pounds bone-in pork shoulder (Boston butt), cut into 8 pieces by your butcher

¼ cup freshly squeezed orange juice

¼ cup freshly squeezed lime juice

2 ounces achiote paste

1 tablespoon dried oregano

2 tablespoons vegetable oil

TOTAL COOK TIME

2 hours, plus 1 hour marinating time

TIP

Achiote paste (annatto) is available in Caribbean and Mexican groceries and many large supermarkets.

PORK RIBS IN HIBISCUS SAUCE
(Costillas en Salsa de Jamaica)

This recipe is a more elaborate—and arguably, even better—version of our Pork Chops with Hibiscus Salsa (page 80). Here, the salsa is augmented with other spices and cooked for nine hours, then served over garlicky summer squash. Despite the long cooking time, this feels like a fast recipe since most of it is unattended—the oven does most of the work.

We created this recipe for our first collaboration at our restaurant Veracruz Fonda & Bar with Deepa Shridhar, a chef who specializes in South Indian–Texan flavors. The event was held in October in honor of the beginning of Día de los Muertos, so we wanted to highlight ingredients that were significant to us, but that would also be appealing to an Indian palate. We named our collaboration El Ritual, to honor the ritual that cooking is for all of us. The ribs were transformed into a beautiful, flavorful taco served on a roti tortilla. It was the best of both worlds.

1. To make the Jamaica seasoning for the ribs, heat the oven to 350°F. On a rimmed baking sheet, place the hibiscus in a single layer and bake for 10 minutes. Cool to room temperature, then grind to a fine powder in a spice grinder or small food processor. In a small bowl, combine the powder, salt, paprika, pepper, onion powder, and garlic powder.

2. If the butcher hasn't already done so, using a sharp knife pointed away from you, remove the silverskin—the papery layer covering one side of the ribs. (Hold the ribs with a paper towel and a firm grip.) Pat the ribs dry and rub evenly with 2 tablespoons of the Jamaica seasoning, then pat the remaining Jamaica seasoning evenly on the meaty side of the ribs. Wrap the ribs in plastic and refrigerate for at least 12 hours and up to 24 hours.

3. Heat the oven to 250°F. In a large bowl, combine the zucchini, salsa, garlic, onion, jalapeños, cilantro, lard, salt, and pepper. Spread these ingredients in a roasting pan and place the ribs on top of a wire rack, if available. Nestle a ramekin in the corner of the pan and fill it with the vinegar and ¼ cup water (this is important to keep a humid environment for the ribs).

4. Cover the pan with aluminum foil, carefully transfer it to the oven (so the vinegar doesn't spill), and bake for 8 hours. Uncover and baste with more salsa, turn the oven temperature up to 350°F, and bake, uncovered, for 1 hour longer. Serve hot.

SERVES 4

FOR THE JAMAICA SEASONING:

2½ tablespoons flor de Jamaica (dried hibiscus flowers)

1 tablespoon kosher salt

1 tablespoon paprika

1½ teaspoons freshly ground black pepper

1½ teaspoons onion powder

1 teaspoon garlic powder

FOR THE RIBS:

1½ racks (4 to 4½ pounds) St. Louis–style pork ribs

2 pounds zucchini or yellow squash, cut into roughly 2-inch chunks

2 tablespoons Hibiscus Salsa (page 78), plus more for basting

10 garlic cloves, minced

1 medium white onion, sliced

2 jalapeño chiles, stemmed and minced

½ packed cup fresh cilantro leaves, minced

¼ cup pork lard or extra-virgin olive oil

2 teaspoons kosher salt

1½ teaspoons freshly ground black pepper

¼ cup apple cider vinegar

TOTAL COOK TIME

9 hours, plus 12 hours marinating time

TIP

We use this Jamaica seasoning in Beef and Cactus Paddles (page 197), but you will likely find other uses for its tart, deep flavor—it even makes a good rim for margaritas and other cocktails.

VERACRUZANO CHICKEN STEW
(Estofado de Pollo)

This dish has always been one of the top three favorites in our family, passed down from generation to generation and beloved by everyone. We all make our own version: Maritza, for example, leaves out the bay leaf and pepper, and she adds more chipotles plus some butter to enrich the sauce. Maritza's daughter, Lis, makes it with cubed chicken breast and serves it in a bowl over rice. Reyna loves eating with her hands, and she re-dips the bones in the sauce.

Embrace this adaptability and create your own family favorite. Use chicken parts instead of a whole chicken, use other kinds of potatoes, and adjust the ingredient quantities to taste. Make the dish extra saucy by adding more tomato and water, or cook the sauce down so it's extra-thick. Some cooks in Veracruz add seasonings like thyme, oregano, allspice, or canela (Mexican cinnamon), and even capers, olives, raisins, and almonds.

1. Mince the garlic, salt, and pepper until it becomes a paste. In a large bowl, combine the paste with 1 tablespoon water. Pat the chicken dry and add it to the bowl, rubbing the seasoning onto all surfaces of the chicken. Let it sit at room temperature for 20 minutes. Wipe the marinade from the chicken before cooking, reserving it for later.

2. In your widest deep skillet or Dutch oven, heat the oil over medium-high heat. Working in batches if necessary, add the chicken in a single layer and cook until deeply brown on all sides, about 10 minutes total. Transfer the chicken to a large platter as it is done. When all the chicken is cooked, add the potatoes to the pan and let them cook in the chicken fat, stirring occasionally, until they begin to brown on all sides, about 3 minutes. Add the reserved marinade, stir to coat the potatoes, then transfer to the plate with the chicken.

3. Add ¼ cup water to the pan, scraping up any browned bits, then add the tomatoes, onion, bay leaves, chipotles, and 1½ cups water. Stir well, then return the chicken and potatoes to the pan. Cook for about 15 minutes, or just until the potatoes are soft and the chicken is cooked through when you cut into the thickest part of a thigh. Taste the sauce and add salt and/or more adobo from the can, if needed. Serve immediately on its own, or over rice.

SERVES 4

18 garlic cloves, peeled

1 tablespoon kosher salt

1 teaspoon freshly ground black pepper

1 (5-pound) whole chicken, cut into 10 pieces

3 tablespoons extra-virgin olive oil

1½ pounds Yukon Gold potatoes, cut into 1-inch dice

8 Roma tomatoes, diced, juices reserved

1 large white onion, diced (about 3 cups)

7 dried bay leaves

2 canned chipotle chiles in adobo (or to taste), minced

White Rice (page 46), for serving (optional)

TOTAL COOK TIME

1 hour

BLACK MOLE
FROM MAMA'S KITCHEN
(*Mole Negro de Nuestra Mamá*)

When our mom got married, she was only sixteen and moved from Veracruz to Puebla with her husband's family. She had watched her mother make mole growing up, and she watched with interest as her new mother-in-law made it, too. She soon developed her own version, taking care not to use too many spices or too many hot chiles, because spicy moles upset our grandfather's stomach, and she wanted him to enjoy it. By the age of twenty-five, she says she had perfected her mole recipe. At first, she'd make it only on special occasions, but eventually she discovered that it could be a way to make money for our family by selling it at our home restaurant. When we were kids, the smell of mole would wake us up every weekend—the sweetest alarm. We knew it meant that it was time to help with Mom's fonda service. We looked forward to that because we knew we'd be eating enmoladas (see page 153) or mole picaditas (see page 42) that day.

Have all the ingredients measured and within reach before starting to cook. This is important for any recipe, but especially key here because this recipe, while not technically difficult, calls for many ingredients that cook relatively quickly, and that are added at different times. Having them at the ready will help you remember what you already added, and ensure that ingredients don't burn while you're retrieving or measuring other ingredients.

Animal crackers, called galletas de animalitos in Mexico, have been popular in Mexico since the early 1900s. They are a common ingredient in moles, even in commercial brands. They add a touch of sweetness while helping thicken the sauce.

SERVES 6

¾ cup vegetable oil, divided, plus more as needed

11 ancho chiles, stemmed and seeded

5 pasilla chiles, stemmed and seeded

2 morita chiles, stemmed

1½ tablespoons pepitas (pumpkin seeds)

2 tablespoons toasted peanuts

2 tablespoons raisins

2 garlic cloves, peeled

5 whole cloves

½ teaspoon cumin seeds

½ teaspoon black peppercorns

¼ cup chopped white onion

½ cup animal crackers (any brand)

1 piece crusty bread, about 2 inches square

½ corn tortilla

⅓ cup toasted sesame seeds

6½ cups Chicken Broth (page 57) or Vegetable Broth (page 55), or store-bought divided, plus more if needed

3 ounces Mexican chocolate (such as Taza, Ibarra, or Abuelita brands; see Tips)

2 ounces piloncillo or 2 packed tablespoons dark brown sugar

1 (2-inch) stick canela (Mexican, or Ceylon, cinnamon)

4½ pounds bone-in chicken pieces

Corn Tortillas (page 39) or store-bought and White Rice (page 46), for serving

TOTAL COOK TIME
2½ hours

1. In a Dutch oven, heat $1/2$ cup of the oil over medium-high heat. Working in batches, add the ancho, pasilla, and morita chiles and cook for 10 to 15 seconds, just until they are pliable and aromatic. Transfer the chiles to a large bowl as you cook.

2. Turn the heat down to medium and add the pumpkin seeds, cooking until they brown and start to pop, 3 to 4 minutes. Use a slotted spoon to transfer them to the bowl with the chiles. Add the peanuts, raisins, garlic, cloves, cumin seeds, and peppercorns and cook until the peanuts are brown but not yet burned, about 3 minutes. As you cook the ingredients, add more oil, if needed, to keep the bottom of the pan coated with hot oil. Transfer to the bowl. Add the onion and cook until it turns dark brown, about 5 minutes, then transfer to the bowl. Add the animal crackers, bread, and tortilla and cook until golden brown, about 3 minutes, then transfer to the bowl. Add the sesame seeds to the bowl.

3. In a small saucepan, bring 5 cups of the broth to a boil. Pour it into the bowl of fried ingredients and let soak for 10 minutes. Transfer to a blender in two or three batches and puree until it becomes very smooth (at least 2 minutes on high). Transfer to another large bowl. At the end, add another 1 cup broth to the blender to dislodge any chile paste that's hard to get out, and add to the bowl.

4. Rinse and dry the Dutch oven. Drizzle in the remaining $1/4$ cup oil and heat over medium-high heat. Add the puréed mixture all at once. Bring it to a boil, then add the chocolate, piloncillo, and canela. Stir until the chocolate and piloncillo dissolve, then add the remaining $1/2$ cup broth (more if it seems too thick; it should be the consistency of heavy cream).

5. Add the chicken, partly cover the pan, and cook until it is cooked through, about 45 minutes (check the dark meat with a knife or use a meat thermometer to cook to 165°F). Taste and add more salt or piloncillo, if needed. Add more broth to thin the mole, or let it evaporate for a few minutes to thicken. Serve with tortillas and rice.

TIPS

Mexican chocolate is easy to find in large supermarkets, Mexican groceries, and online. It has seasonings such as canela (Mexican cinnamon) and a different texture than other chocolate, but in a pinch you can substitute any dark chocolate.

To make this gluten-free, add an extra $1\frac{1}{2}$ tortillas and an extra tablespoon of piloncillo in place of the bread and animal crackers.

CREAMY POBLANO CHICKEN
(Pollo a la Crema)

Roasted poblano chiles and Mexican crema are a match made in heaven. Substituting coconut milk for part of the crema is a nice way to add another layer of flavor while also limiting the amount of dairy in this recipe, which can feel heavy on the palate when used in large quantities.

1. Mince the garlic, salt, and pepper together until it becomes a paste. In a large bowl, rub all over the chicken and set aside for 10 minutes at room temperature, or cover and refrigerate for up to 24 hours.

2. While the chicken marinates, roast the poblanos by placing them directly over a gas flame or under a broiler. Turn them often until their skin is blackened but not disintegrated, then place them in a ziplock bag or covered bowl for at least 5 minutes. When cool enough to handle, gently peel and discard the charred skin (it's OK if some remains), then make a lengthwise slit and carefully remove and discard the seeds, veins, and stems. Slice into thin strips and set aside.

3. In a large, deep skillet, heat the oil over medium heat. Add the chicken and cook until it turns golden brown, 3 to 5 minutes per side. Add the onion, serrano, and roasted poblanos. Cook, stirring occasionally, for 3 minutes, then add the crema, coconut milk, and salt to taste. Cook until the sauce is bubbly and thick and the chicken is cooked through, about 5 minutes longer. Serve right away with rice.

SERVES 4

5 garlic cloves, peeled

1½ teaspoons kosher salt

1 teaspoon freshly ground black pepper

1½ pounds boneless, skinless chicken breasts, cut into 1-inch strips

2 large poblano chiles

2 tablespoons extra-virgin olive oil

½ medium white onion, thinly sliced

1 serrano chile, stemmed and thinly sliced

1 cup Mexican crema

1 cup unsweetened coconut milk

White Rice (page 46), for serving

TOTAL COOK TIME

45 minutes

TIP

You can roast and peel the poblanos in advance; they will keep in a tightly covered container in the refrigerator for up to 4 days or in the freezer for up to 6 months.

CHICKEN IN RED PUMPKIN-SEED SAUCE
(Pollo con Pipián Rojo)

This sauce rivals the complexity of Oaxaca's famed mole negro (see our mom's version on page 210) and is a favorite in Veracruz (where it's often called tlatonile), even though it's little known outside the state. It's an impressive, festive entrée when served with rice, tortillas, and plantains. You can also pull the chicken from the bones and mix it with the sauce to use as a taco filling or a topping for Picadas (page 42). Or feel free to make the sauce on its own to mix with any meat or veggies.

1. To make the chicken, in a large pot, combine 4 quarts water with the onion, garlic, and salt and bring to a boil over high heat. Add the chicken and return the water to a boil. Turn the heat down to medium and cook until the chicken thighs are cooked through, about 30 minutes. Skim off any foam that rises to the surface during cooking. Drain the chicken and set aside.

2. Meanwhile, to make the pipián, in a large saucepan, bring 3 quarts water to a boil over high heat. Add the moritas and cook for 25 minutes, then add the tomatoes and cook for 20 minutes longer.

3. While the chiles and tomatoes cook, in a large skillet over medium heat, toast the anchos, turning once or twice, until they are fragrant but not charred, about 1 minute. Add to the pan with the chiles and tomatoes.

4. In the skillet used for the anchos, cook the pepitas, stirring often, until they change color and start to pop, about 5 minutes. Transfer to a bowl. Toast the sesame seeds, cloves, cumin seeds, and canela in the pan, stirring often, until the seeds are golden, about 5 minutes. Transfer to the bowl with the pepitas.

5. Working in batches as necessary, in a blender, add the chile and tomato mixture, the seed mixture, the onion, garlic, and salt. Pulse until it's almost smooth; you want to retain some granular texture from the pepitas. Add a little water, if needed, to keep the blades turning. Transfer the mixture to a large bowl.

6. In a large pot or Dutch oven, heat the oil over medium heat. Add the blender mixture (careful, it will splatter) and cook, stirring constantly, for 1 minute. Add the broth and stir well, then add the reserved chicken pieces. Let the chicken cook for 5 minutes, adding more broth, if needed, for a consistency of heavy cream. Taste and add more salt, if needed. Serve right away.

SERVES 4

FOR THE CHICKEN:

1 medium white onion, quartered

12 garlic cloves, halved

1½ tablespoons kosher salt

1 (5-pound) whole chicken, cut into 10 pieces

FOR THE PIPIÁN:

4 dried morita or chipotle chiles, stemmed and seeded

1 pound Roma tomatoes

5 ounces ancho chiles (about 12), stemmed and seeded

2 cups pepitas (pumpkin seeds)

⅓ cup sesame seeds

2 whole cloves

¼ teaspoon whole cumin seeds

1 stick canela (Mexican, or Ceylon, cinnamon)

¼ small white onion

5 garlic cloves

¼ cup extra-virgin olive oil

2 teaspoons kosher salt

2 cups Chicken Broth (page 57) or store-bought

White Rice (page 46), Fried Plantains (page 95), and Corn Tortillas (page 39), or store-bought, for serving

TOTAL COOK TIME

1½ hours

ACHIOTE CHICKEN
(Pollo en Achiote)

If it were up to me (Reyna), I'd cook everything with achiote. It's one of my favorite spices to use with any kind of meat, but my favorite protein with achiote—with apologies to cochinita pibil—is chicken. In the Veracruz mercados, most butcher shops sell meat already marinating in some kind of achiote paste.

When my mom had a butcher shop, we siblings were responsible for receiving, killing, cleaning, and butchering the chickens. When sales were slow, we knew that if we offered some chickens already seasoned with this marinade, they'd sell fast. Every time I share this recipe, it takes me back to that butcher shop!

1. To make the chicken, in a large bowl, place the chicken. In a blender, combine the orange juice, garlic, achiote seeds, oil, coriander seeds, salt, and pepper and blend until smooth. Using gloves or a spoon since it will stain your fingers, coat the chicken evenly with the achiote paste. Let the chicken sit at room temperature for 1 hour, or cover and refrigerate for up to 24 hours.

2. Heat the oven to 425°F. Place the chicken in a single layer on a rimmed baking sheet and roast for about 30 minutes, or until the thickest part of the thigh reads 165°F on a meat thermometer (or cut into the thigh to make sure it's no longer raw against the bone).

3. Meanwhile, to make the pickled onions, in a small bowl, toss the onion, serranos, lime juice, pepper, and salt until they are well combined. Taste and add more salt, if needed. Cover and refrigerate until ready to use (no more than 6 hours).

4. Serve the chicken hot, with the escabeche on top or added separately.

SERVES 4

FOR THE CHICKEN:

3 pounds bone-in, skin-on chicken thighs (see Note)

¾ cup freshly squeezed orange juice

8 garlic cloves, peeled

3 tablespoons achiote seeds

2 tablespoons extra-virgin olive oil

2 teaspoons coriander seeds

1½ teaspoons kosher salt

½ teaspoon freshly ground black pepper

FOR THE PICKLED ONIONS (ESCABECHE):

1 medium white onion, very thinly sliced

2 serrano chiles, stemmed, seeded, if desired, and minced

¼ cup freshly squeezed lime juice

1 teaspoon freshly ground black pepper

½ teaspoon kosher salt

TOTAL COOK TIME

45 minutes, plus 1 hour marinating time

NOTE

Bone-in chicken thighs vary widely in size and weight. Be sure there are at least two thighs per person here, even if it means buying more than 3 pounds.

FRIED CHICKEN
(Pollo Frito)

This fried chicken recipe comes from our maternal grandmother, Cecilia. She rarely cooked—not because she didn't know how, but because she had twelve kids and had to work, so her daughters—our aunts—would usually do the cooking. She would, however, cook on her one free day a week, and she would usually make pollo frito. I don't know if it was because we all loved it so much, or if it was therapeutic for her—probably both.

If you're up for it, do as she did and boil some new potatoes while the chicken fries, then fry them in the flavorful cooking oil until brown and crispy while the chicken drains. The potatoes will take only a few minutes to cook and are spectacular.

Each time she made this dish, Celia would remind us, "El pollo siempre tiene que tener suficiente ajo o no sabe igual" (the chicken won't taste the same without enough garlic) and it's true: This recipe can't have enough garlic. The overnight marinade ensures intense garlic flavor.

1. Mince the garlic, salt, and pepper together until it becomes a paste. In a large bowl, mix the paste with 2 tablespoons water. Pat the chicken dry and add it to the bowl, rubbing the seasoning onto all surfaces of the chicken. Cover the bowl and refrigerate for at least 8 hours and up to 24 hours.

2. When ready to cook, sprinkle the paprika evenly over the chicken.

3. In a large Dutch oven or wide deep skillet, add enough oil so that it's about 1½ inches deep—just enough to cover the chicken pieces. (The pan should be large enough to hold all the chicken pieces in a single layer; use two pans if necessary.) Place the pan over medium-high heat until the oil reaches 350°F. Add the chicken pieces and set a timer for 10 minutes.

4. Adjust the heat, if needed, to maintain a temperature between 340°F and 360°F. After 10 minutes, flip the chicken and reset the timer for another 10 minutes. After these 10 minutes, check the chicken with a meat thermometer—it should be at least 165°F at the thickest part near the bone. Drain the chicken on a rack (not paper towels) and serve hot with rice, beans, and both salsas.

SERVES 4

1 head garlic, cloves separated and peeled (about 12 cloves)

1 tablespoon kosher salt

1 teaspoon freshly ground black pepper

1 (5-pound) whole chicken, cut into 10 pieces, or 4 to 5 pounds bone-in, skin-on chicken parts of your choice

1½ tablespoons paprika

Vegetable oil, for deep-frying (about 8 cups)

White Rice (page 46) or Mexican Rice (page 47), Black Beans (page 49) or Refried Beans (page 49), Creamy Jalapeño Salsa (page 73), and Spicy Citrus Salsa (page 77), for serving

TOTAL COOK TIME

45 minutes, plus 8 hours marinating time

TIP

Although we suggest serving this dish with rice and beans, you can, of course, serve this with any side dishes you like—or none at all. Do try to have both salsas at the table, though—the combination turns a platter of fried chicken into something extra-special.

ROAST CHICKEN
(Pollo Rostizado)

There's a charcoal-roasted chicken chain in Mexico called El Pollo Feliz, and going there was always a special outing for the family. It was fascinating to see how these restaurants operated, serving so many people so quickly while maintaining impressive quality in their chicken, tortillas, and salsas. They now have more than 850 locations in Mexico, so they're doing something right! This recipe is inspired by them. Make sure to dip your potatoes and carrots in the juice that the chicken releases at the bottom of the pan.

1. Heat the oven to 400°F.

2. In a small bowl, mix together the butter, onion, garlic, salt, paprika, and pepper until uniform. Pat the chicken dry. Using a sharp knife or scissors, make several cuts in the skin without piercing the meat. Make cuts where the thighs and wings meet the breast, so that your fingers can pass under the breast skin. Using your hands, coat the chicken with the butter mixture, using about half of the mixture under the skin and half on the skin, and saving a little to smear in the cavity.

3. In a shallow roasting pan, spread the potatoes and carrots in a single layer. Place the chicken on top, cover it with aluminum foil, and roast for about 1¹/₂ hours, or until a meat thermometer in the thickest part of the thigh reaches 165°F. Let the chicken sit for at least 10 minutes before serving.

SERVES 4

1 stick (8 tablespoons) unsalted butter, at room temperature

¹/₂ medium red onion, minced

8 garlic cloves, minced

1 tablespoon kosher salt

1 tablespoon paprika

2 teaspoons freshly ground black pepper

1 (4- to 5-pound) whole chicken

2 large russet potatoes, peeled, cut into 2-inch chunks

3 large carrots, peeled, cut into 2-inch chunks

TOTAL COOK TIME

2 hours

TIP

For extra flavor, marinate the butter-coated chicken for up to 24 hours in the refrigerator.

CHIPOTLE-STEWED CHICKEN
(Tinga de Pollo)

Tinga was always present at family parties, and we'd make it in huge quantities, stretching it out with shredded cabbage, since it was often the most popular dish. It's great on tostadas, in tacos, on Picadas (page 42), as a filling for chiles rellenos, and alongside White Rice (page 46). You can even eat it at room temperature (or straight out of the fridge). We usually serve it on a platter next to tostadas, shredded lettuce, crumbled queso fresco, and Refried Beans (page 49) for people to make their own tostadas.

1. In a medium saucepan, place the chicken, 1 garlic clove, half the onion, the salt, and 6 cups water. Bring to a boil over high heat and cook for 20 minutes. Transfer the chicken to a plate, then strain the cooking liquid into a large bowl and set aside.

2. While the chicken cools, in a blender, combine the remaining 3 garlic cloves, the tomatoes, 3 of the chipotles, the ketchup, and the oregano and blend until smooth. When the chicken is cool enough to handle, pull it into thick shreds with your hands or with two forks and return it to the pan.

3. In a medium skillet, heat the oil over medium heat. Add the remaining onion and cook, stirring occasionally, until it becomes translucent, about 3 minutes. Add the blended tomato mixture and bay leaves and cook, stirring occasionally, for 3 minutes. While it's cooking, add 1½ cups of the reserved chicken cooking liquid to the blender, blend briefly to incorporate any leftover tomato mixture, and add it to the pan, along with the chicken. Cook until the sauce is the texture you want—some people like it coating the chicken thickly, some people like a soupier texture; we like it somewhere in between, so there's plenty of sauce to soak up, but it's still clinging to the chicken. Add salt, if needed, and stir in the 3 remaining chipotles. Serve right away.

SERVES 4 TO 6

2 pounds boneless, skinless chicken breasts

4 garlic cloves, peeled, divided

1½ medium white onions, chopped, divided

2 teaspoons kosher salt, plus more as needed

4 Roma tomatoes, quartered

6 canned chipotle chiles in adobo, divided

2 tablespoons ketchup

2½ teaspoons dried oregano

3 tablespoons extra-virgin olive oil

2 dried bay leaves

TOTAL COOK TIME

45 minutes

TIP

To extend this recipe inexpensively for a larger group while also adding flavor and fiber, add 2 cups finely shredded cabbage when you start sautéing the onion.

8
SOMETHING SWEET

"Si la vida no es dulce, endúlzala tu mismo."

(IF LIFE ISN'T SWEET, SWEETEN IT YOURSELF.)

The first thing you'll see when you enter our full-service brick-and-mortar restaurant, Veracruz Fonda & Bar, is a wall-size triptych mural of a beautiful woman with an intense gaze. The woman is María Félix, an icon of the Golden Age of Mexican cinema in the 1940s and 1950s, and whose legacy in the worlds of film, fashion, music, art, and literature still stands today. Along with her powerful cinematic presence, she's known for being audaciously outspoken, fearless, and very progressive. Her life was full of turmoil; still, she insisted on working and living on her own daring terms and empowered women by pushing boundaries that few dared to question at the time.

AS KIDS WHOSE PARENTS LOVED her movies, we knew that she was a woman who never let anyone walk all over her. We didn't recognize it at the time, but looking back, we realize that many of the women in our lives were influencing us. Women who didn't conform to the norms that society placed on them. Hardworking women like María who challenged the "rules" gave us our idea of independence and self-sufficiency. She, like many others, including our grandmothers and aunts, became the people whom we identified with and admired, especially as business owners. Through role models like these, we recognized the strength that our mother passed down to us, giving us the courage to go after anything we wanted.

We love that our mural shows the different sides of María Félix, from the girly-girl to the working woman with a smoke and a sombrero. She was a chameleon of a woman, and her mercurial temperament contributed to her strength. At a time when women were often objectified and minimized, she showcased every facet of being a woman in the fifty films she starred in and the independent life she led over her eighty-eight years.

We walk past that mural almost every day, and it is a constant reminder of all those women who paved the way for us—that we are free to be who we want to be at any point of our life, that our dreams are unbound. It also reminds us of the strength and courage we carry in our genes. Veracruz All Natural is, of course, an homage to another powerful woman who inspired us: our mother. She was, and still is, a paragon of resilience and strength.

MAMA'S BREAD PUDDING
(Budín de Mamá)

As kids, we'd usually had fresh bolillo (crusty bread) to drink with coffee. Smothering the bread in butter and either sugar, jam, or condensed milk was a way to have pan dulce (sweet bread) with coffee without having to buy pastries from a bakery. When there was leftover bread that had gone stale, Mom's budín would appear on our dinner table. Neither of us has a big sweet tooth, but this gently sweet budín suits our tastes, and it's a simple dish that remains one of our favorite desserts to this day.

Feel free to substitute nondairy milk for the whole milk here; just know that you then lose the privilege of crediting it to our mom! The serving yield isn't a joke: Some people might want a small portion of this, but we find it hard not to eat the whole thing in one sitting.

1. Heat the oven to 350°F. Grease a 9 x 9-inch baking dish.

2. In a large bowl, combine the bread, milk, and 1 cup water, pushing the bread into the liquid with your hand. Let the bread soak for 30 minutes. Add the butter, sugar, vanilla, and cinnamon and mix until well combined. Mix in the raisins, distributing them equally throughout.

3. Transfer the batter to the baking dish and bake for 55 minutes. It should be firm and hot throughout when it is finished. Serve warm or at room temperature.

SERVES 2 TO 8

1 baguette, cut into 10 slices

2½ cups whole milk

6 tablespoons unsalted butter, melted

½ cup packed light brown sugar

½ teaspoon vanilla extract

½ teaspoon ground cinnamon

¼ cup raisins

TOTAL COOK TIME

1½ hours

REYNA'S CONCHA QUEST

Our grandfather was one of the best bakers in town, and several uncles were bakers as well. It was fun when our grandfather would show up at our house on weekend afternoons, maybe a little tipsy with his sombrero cocked to one side, carrying a bag of sweet breads. We'd wait with Grandma with black coffee ready for him, then we'd dive into the bag, going for the conchas first.

With my conchas, I wanted to create something new, not copy. I wanted to be able to say this was my mine and that I made this recipe from beginning to end, with no help and no guide, just created from memory. I wanted to re-create the conchas that I remembered so fondly: the gently sweet flavor and soft texture of Grandpa's conchas. Memory is complicated, though, and fickle. But food awakens and sharpens it; food evokes sense memories that your body remembers even when your mind doesn't. In the case of the conchas, I wasn't sure what I was going for technically, but I was confident that my taste buds would know when I got it right.

However, unlike our grandfather, I wanted to make conchas with whole wheat flour and butter, rather than the all-white flour and vegetable shortening that most Mexican bakeries use. Butter, I figured, would help them stay soft and moist longer than those made with shortening, which can get hard and dry within hours. To complicate things further, there are subtle differences in the milk and sugar we grew up with, making me wonder if maybe the whole exercise was futile.

In the end, I worked on this recipe on and off for at least three years, with hundreds of delicious—but not quite perfect—conchas along the way. I began creating it when my grandfather passed away, and in the process of perfecting it, my grandmother followed him. This recipe is at once a tribute to my grandparents—it bears my grandfather's trademark pillowy texture, but, at the same time, it's also my recipe, and now one of the most popular all-day sweets at our restaurant—and a new family tradition.

WHOLE WHEAT CONCHAS
(Conchas Integrales)

Conchas are not-too-sweet buns that are equally good for breakfast, a midday snack, or dessert. For the latter, try sandwiching them with whipped cream, pastry cream, or ice cream. Unlike most of the recipes in this book, this recipe isn't particularly simple, fast, or forgiving, but we hope you'll make it, since the process (and end product) is incredibly rewarding. It's possible to make this with 100 percent whole wheat flour, though they'll be denser with an earthier flavor. To do so, try to find whole wheat bread flour, and add an additional quarter cup milk to the masa madre (starter), as whole wheat flour absorbs more liquid than white flour.

We used weight as a measurement here instead of volume because precise measurements are so important in baking yeasted breads. We're choosing not to include cup measurements because we want your conchas to be perfect. You can find conversions online, but you can purchase a kitchen scale for less than $10, and we're certain that you'll find other uses for it as well.

1. To make the starter, in a medium saucepan, heat the milk over low heat until it reaches 140°F. Add the milk to the bowl of a stand mixer, along with the yeast, bread flour, and sugar. Using the whisk attachment, whisk for 30 seconds on medium speed. When it starts to foam, remove the whisk attachment, cover the bowl with plastic wrap, and let it sit for 20 minutes. (If not using a stand mixer, just use a whisk here.)

2. To make the conchas, to the same saucepan that you used for the milk, melt the butter over low heat so that it's completely soft but it doesn't separate; it should stay a creamy yellow color. Set aside.

3. Add the bread flour to the mixer bowl with the starter and, using the paddle attachment, start beating the flour on low speed. Add about a third of the eggs and a third of the butter (it's OK if it's a little more or less than a third). Mix for about 20 seconds, until combined, then add half of the whole wheat flour, another third of the eggs, and another third of the butter. Mix for about 20 seconds, then add the remaining whole wheat flour, eggs, and butter. Add the granulated sugar, cinnamon, vanilla, and salt and mix for 30 seconds, until it forms a uniform dough. (If not using a stand mixer, use a wooden spoon, mixing very well after each addition.)

MAKES 12 TO 16 CONCHAS

FOR THE STARTER:

½ cup whole milk

10 grams rapid-rise yeast

2 tablespoons white bread flour

1 tablespoon granulated sugar

FOR THE CONCHAS:

200 grams unsalted butter, cut into ½-inch cubes

340 grams white bread flour, sifted

285 grams beaten eggs (about 5)

340 grams whole wheat flour, sifted

175 grams granulated sugar

2 teaspoons ground cinnamon

1 teaspoon vanilla extract

¼ teaspoon kosher salt

½ teaspoon oil (any type)

FOR THE TOPS:

140 grams unsalted butter, at room temperature

140 grams sifted powdered sugar

140 grams white bread flour

2 teaspoons ground cinnamon

TOTAL COOK TIME

1 hour, plus 3 hours resting time

4. Switch to the dough hook attachment (removing the excess dough from the paddle attachment) and knead on medium speed for 10 minutes. (If not using a stand mixer, knead manually for at least 10 minutes.)

5. While the dough is being kneaded, coat a large mixing bowl with the oil. Add the dough in a ball (tuck the sides under to help it keep a ball shape with a taut top), cover with plastic wrap, and leave at room temperature for 2 hours.

6. To make the tops while the dough rests, in a bowl, add the butter, powdered sugar, flour, and cinnamon and mix with your hands until it has a uniform texture similar to Play-Doh. Form into a ball, cover with plastic wrap, and place in a cool area (use the refrigerator if your room is warm).

7. Line two rimmed baking sheet with parchment paper. Uncover the dough and punch gently to deflate. Divide the dough into 12 to 16 equal pieces, depending on how many people you're feeding and the desired size of the finished conchas. Shape each into a smooth round ball and place them on the prepared baking sheets, spacing them evenly.

8. Divide the sugar dough topping into the same number as the conchas. Press each portion using a tortilla press or rolling them between sheets of plastic or parchment into rounds big enough to cover the dough balls without having to tuck them underneath (you want to cover all the visible parts of the dough balls since they will rise further).

9. Using a sharp knife or pizza cutter, slice five curved lines through the sugar tops, radiating from one point (to look like a seashell). You want to cut through the sugar tops without cutting into the dough. There are concha cutters you can buy for this purpose.

10. Cover the pans loosely with cheesecloth or with thin dish towels. Let them sit until the conchas double in size. The time will vary with the temperature of the room, but this process usually takes about 1 hour.

11. Heat the oven to 350°F. If you have a fan option on your oven, turn it on, but if not, it's OK.

12. Place the conchas in the oven for 14 minutes. Check the bottoms, which should be golden brown; if not, return the sheets to the oven for a couple more minutes. Cool on a wire rack and serve.

VARIATIONS:

CHOCOLATE: For the tops, replace the cinnamon with ¼ cup cocoa powder.

CITRUS: For the concha dough, replace the cinnamon with 1 packed tablespoon grated citrus zest (orange works well). For the tops, replace the cinnamon with 1 packed tablespoon grated citrus zest.

PECAN: Add ½ cup very finely chopped pecans each to the dough and the tops (1 cup total).

BLUE CORN: For the tops, omit the cinnamon and replace half of the flour with blue corn masa harina.

CHEESE FLAN
(Flan de Queso)

I (Maritza) clearly remember the Christmas when I was nine. Our father was always trying out DIY projects, and that winter, he had just built a room off our kitchen. As we were getting ready to sit down to dinner and celebrate with family, it began to pour. The addition, which, so far had proven to be sturdy, funneled a river of rainwater into our kitchen, ruining the evening.

I only saw that we had an indoor pool in the house, but it was clear that this wasn't a happy moment. Our aunt, Tía Estela, picked me up, gently set me on the counter, and said "Vamos a hacer un flan." *Let's make a flan.* She explained, step by step, what the flan included, and I followed along without missing a single step or ingredient. As she took it out of the baño maría (bain-marie, or water bath), I inhaled the sweet smell of the caramel and vanilla that filled the room; it's an aroma I will never forget, and to this day, flan reminds me not of a flooded house and frantic holiday, but instead one of the sweetest moments of my childhood. Many years later, Tía Estela came to visit us in Texas and made the flan again for my kids and me. It tasted just as sweet and full of love as the first time.

1. Heat the oven to 350°F. Have ready a 7^1/$_2$-inch flan pan or an 8-inch round pie or cake pan, as well as a deep roasting pan or casserole dish large enough to hold the flan pan.

2. In a medium skillet, add the sugar and cook over medium-low heat until it melts and turns a dark golden brown. As the sugar melts, move the pan by rotating it, rather than stirring with a spoon or other implement. Caramel cooks quickly once it starts changing color, so don't step away from the stove while it's cooking. Transfer the caramel to the flan pan and immediately rotate it to coat the bottom and about an inch up the sides (you can also use a heatproof pastry brush to assist). Set aside.

3. Bring a small saucepan of water to a boil. Meanwhile, in a blender, add the condensed milk, evaporated milk, cream cheese, eggs, and vanilla and blend until smooth. Pour the mixture into the flan pan and cover with a lid or aluminum foil. Place the flan pan inside the larger roasting pan, then place both in the oven on the center rack. Pour enough boiling water into the roasting pan to reach about halfway up the sides of the flan pan. Take care not to get any water in the flan pan itself.

SERVES 8

½ cup sugar

1 (14-ounce) can condensed milk

1 (12-ounce) can evaporated milk

8 ounces cream cheese

5 large eggs

1 teaspoon vanilla extract

TOTAL COOK TIME

2 hours

4. Bake for 1 hour 20 minutes, then remove from the oven. Transfer the flan pan to a wire rack and allow it to cool for at least 10 minutes. Run a butter knife around the edge of the pan to loosen, then place a flat serving plate upside-down over the top of the pan and flip it over quickly so the flan and its caramel sauce unmold and land upright on the plate. Do this over the sink, since some caramel sauce may dribble out when you flip it over. Let it cool for at least 15 minutes before serving, or cover it with plastic or foil and refrigerate until you're ready to serve.

COCONUT-MEZCAL ICE CREAM
(Helado de Coco y Mezcal)

Although mezcal is now easy to find in Mexico and the US, it's something we've only known as adults; when we left Mexico as teenagers, it wasn't a common spirit in Veracruz. We think that its smoky flavor pairs beautifully with coconut, an essential flavor in the sweet treats of Veracruz. If you don't want to fight with a whole coconut, you can use 2 cups dried unsweetened coconut (be sure it's 100 percent coconut). You can often find frozen fresh grated coconut in Indian groceries. You'll need an ice cream maker for our ice creams, but it's a worthwhile investment even if you just plan to make ice cream a few times a year.

1. In a large skillet, add the coconut and cook over medium-high heat, stirring often, just until it starts to change color, about 5 minutes. Remove the pan from the heat, pour the mezcal evenly over the coconut, and light it with a long match or lighter. (If you're nervous about lighting the mezcal on fire, just let it heat through—or take a shot before doing it to calm your nerves!) When the flames subside, return the pan to the heat and cook for 1 minute, stirring occasionally. Transfer the coconut and mezcal mixture to a blender. Wipe the skillet clean and set it aside.

2. In a large mixing bowl, add ice and nestle a smaller bowl inside of it (this will cool your ice cream base later). In another large bowl, whisk the egg yolks and sugar until the sugar dissolves.

3. Add the milk to the coconut mixture in the blender and puree for at least 2 minutes to ensure that the coconut is completely incorporated into the milk. Add the mixture to the skillet and bring to a boil over medium-high heat. When it comes to a boil, pour it very slowly into the yolk mixture, whisking constantly to ensure the yolks don't cook and clump.

4. Pour the resulting mixture through a fine-mesh strainer into the bowl set over ice. Stir in the heavy cream. When cool, freeze according to your ice-cream maker's directions.

MAKES 1 QUART

1 fresh coconut, white meat removed and grated (about 3 cups grated fresh coconut), or 2 cups dried unsweetened coconut

¼ cup mezcal, at room temperature

4 large egg yolks

⅔ cup packed light brown sugar

1½ cups whole milk

1½ cups heavy cream

TOTAL COOK TIME

20 minutes, plus freezing time

STRAWBERRY-BASIL ICE CREAM
(Helado de Fresa y Albahaca)

Basil is a common herb in Veracruz, where the most common type has small leaves, purple stems, and a spicy flavor. Any basil works well here, but if using a different basil than the large-leafed sweet basil most widely available in the US, just use more leaves.

Mexican ice cream tends to be a bit lighter than American ice cream. It's usually made with whole eggs and a higher ratio of milk to cream. Ours is somewhere in between, using egg yolks but with equal parts milk and cream for a less dense texture. Use this ice cream base—¾ cup each milk and cream with 2 egg yolks—to experiment with other fruit-and-herb combinations, adjusting the sugar to taste.

1. In a small saucepan, add the strawberries, 2 tablespoons of the sugar, the basil, lime juice, and 1 teaspoon water, and cook over high heat for 5 minutes; the sugar should dissolve and the strawberries should break down. Transfer to a bowl to cool and set the saucepan aside.

2. In a large mixing bowl, add ice and nestle a smaller bowl inside of it (this will cool your ice cream base later). In another large bowl, whisk the egg yolks and remaining 5 tablespoons sugar until the sugar dissolves.

3. In a blender, add 1 cup of the strawberry mixture with the milk and blend until smooth. Transfer this to the saucepan and bring to a boil over medium-high heat. When it comes to a boil, pour it very slowly into the yolk mixture, whisking constantly to ensure the yolks don't cook and clump.

4. Pour the resulting mixture through a fine-mesh strainer into the bowl set over ice. Stir in the heavy cream. When cool, freeze according to your ice-cream maker's directions.

MAKES 3 CUPS

8 ounces strawberries, hulled and halved

7 tablespoons sugar, divided

4 large basil leaves (about 4 x 2 inches each)

1½ teaspoons freshly squeezed lime juice

2 large egg yolks

¾ cup whole milk

¾ cup heavy cream

TOTAL COOK TIME

20 minutes, plus freezing time

WATERMELON-STRAWBERRY SORBET
(Sorbete de Sandía y Fresa)

We are not "dessert people" in the sense that we don't need a big, sweet dish to end every meal. But we are huge fans of sweet treats. We love sweets that can be enjoyed any time of day, and in Veracruz, as in most of Mexico, paletas (ice pops), raspados (snow cones), sorbetes and nieves (two words for sorbets), and helados (ice creams) fit the bill: They all beat the heat and give you a little boost of energy rather than making you want to nap afterward.

Veracruz is Mexico's second-biggest watermelon-growing state, just behind Sonora. The combination of watermelon and strawberry in this sorbet screams summer. We like to top it with diced fresh strawberries.

In a blender, add the watermelon, strawberries, sugar, and lime juice and blend until smooth. Pass through a fine-mesh strainer into a bowl. Freeze according to your ice-cream maker's directions. Serve topped with additional diced strawberries, if you like.

MAKES 6 CUPS

3 cups diced fresh watermelon, seeds removed

3 cups very ripe strawberries, carefully hulled so as not to waste any of the berry itself, plus diced strawberries, for serving (optional)

¾ cup sugar

¼ cup freshly squeezed lime juice

TOTAL PREPARATION TIME

15 minutes, plus freezing time

ORANGE BREAD
(Pan de Naranja)

Our mom enjoyed having people over for coffee and pan dulce (sweet bread) on leisurely afternoons. Since we didn't have the means to buy pan dulce all the time, she learned to make this bread so we could have something sweet to entertain with. It took a while to formalize this recipe, though, since she used a coffee cup as her measuring cup, and she poked holes in an empty sardine can with a hammer and nails to create an abrasive surface to zest the orange. Her resourcefulness has always been an inspiration.

1. Heat the oven to 375°F. Grease an 8-inch round cake pan. Sprinkle with flour to coat evenly, then tap out any excess.

2. In a large mixing bowl, whisk the flour and baking powder. Whisk in the orange zest and set aside.

3. In the bowl of a stand mixer (or in a large bowl if using a hand mixer), use the whisk attachment to combine the butter and granulated sugar on high speed for about 4 minutes, or until light and fluffy, stopping to scrape down the sides as necessary.

4. Turn the speed down to low and add the eggs one at a time, scraping down the bowl after each addition. Increase the speed to medium and beat for 2 minutes to incorporate more air into the mixture (it will lighten in color). Turn the speed down to low again and add the flour mixture in three parts (so it doesn't escape the bowl), then add the orange juice and milk and beat for another minute.

5. Transfer the batter to the cake pan. Bake for about 45 minutes, or until a toothpick comes out clean (test earlier if you suspect your oven may run hot). Allow the bread to cool on a wire rack, then unmold and dust with powdered sugar through a fine-mesh sieve before serving.

SERVES 8

3½ cups all-purpose flour, plus extra for dusting

1 tablespoon baking powder

1 packed teaspoon grated orange zest, plus ½ cup freshly squeezed orange juice

2½ sticks (20 tablespoons) unsalted butter, at room temperature

1½ cups granulated sugar

4 large eggs

½ cup whole milk

¼ cup sifted powdered sugar

TOTAL COOK TIME

1½ hours

TIP

You can use any nonbitter citrus, such as tangerine, blood orange, or red grapefruit. You can also double this recipe and make it in a decorative Bundt pan (our grandma's favorite).

APPLE TAMALES
(Tamales de Manzana)

I (Reyna) have always loved sweet tamales, but I've never liked the fact that they are usually made with food coloring. I'm a big fan of using natural ingredients to color food: beets, spinach, marigolds, berries. I developed this recipe to enjoy sweet tamales without the added stuff, and it took me a few tries before I could get it right. We recommend serving these for dessert paired with Coconut-Mezcal Ice Cream (page 241). Dried corn husks can be found at any Mexican grocery or online; an eight-ounce package usually contains about fifty husks.

1. To prepare the corn husks, place a large tamale steamer or a stockpot with a steamer insert over high heat and fill it halfway with water. Bring the water to a boil, add the corn husks, turn the heat down to low, and allow it to simmer for at least 15 minutes. With tongs, carefully remove the corn husks from the pot and drain them on dish towels. Reserve the cooking water.

2. Meanwhile, to make the apple filling, in a stand mixer, using the paddle attachment, add the butter and sugar and beat on medium speed for 2 minutes. Increase the speed to high and beat until light and fluffy, about 1 more minute, scraping down the sides as necessary. Turn the speed down to medium, add the masa harina, baking powder, and milk and beat for another 2 minutes. Scrape the sides, then add the apple and pecans. Beat on low speed just until combined.

3. Smear about $\frac{1}{3}$ cup of the apple filling on the wide, bottom half of each drained corn husk, leaving about an inch on either side. Fold both sides toward the middle, fold the empty edges to one side, then fold the "tail" in so that the filling is enclosed with one end open. Repeat the process with the remainder of the filling (you will have corn husks left over).

4. Place 2 leftover corn husks on the bottom of the tamale steamer (or stockpot with steamer insert), add the tamales vertically with the open end up, then cover with about 8 of the remaining husks and a clean cotton dish towel. Cover the pot and place it over medium heat to steam for 45 minutes, at which point the tamales will be cooked through. Serve warm.

5. Store leftover tamales in a tightly covered container in the refrigerator for up to 3 days. Because tamales have no gluten, leftovers reheat beautifully in a microwave, but they can also be reheated in a steamer or on a griddle so that their edges crisp up while they heat through.

MAKES ABOUT 15 TAMALES

30 dried corn husks

2 sticks (16 tablespoons) unsalted butter, at room temperature

1 cup sugar

1½ cups masa harina, such as Mcseca brand

1 teaspoon baking powder

1 cup whole milk

1½ cups finely diced green apple

¼ cup minced pecans

TOTAL COOK TIME

2 hours

9
DRINKS TO START
— OR END —
THE DAY

"De chorrito en chorrito se llena el jarrito."

(DROP BY DROP, THE PITCHER GETS FULL.)

The Mexican version of "slow but steady wins the race" is a sentiment that really resonates with us. Drinks are where we started, selling juices, fruit cups, and raspados (snow cones) from a tiny trailer. Everything we made went right back into the business, and little by little, drop by drop, we slowly outgrew our trailer, turned our business into several taco trucks and now a restaurant that was awarded a Michelin Bib Gourmand award.

JUICES, SMOOTHIES, AND AGUAS FRESCAS bring us back not just to our first outpost, but also to our childhood, where we'd cool off with these cold drinks on hot days or go to the beach and chase down street vendors pushing carts of fruits, juices, paletas (ice pops), and raspados through the sand. Here in Austin, they're delicious, nutritious, and refreshing in the Texas heat, and the various combinations are a way for us to embrace seasonal produce, introduce flavors and flavor combinations from Veracruz, and flex our creativity with new combinations of fruits, vegetables, herbs, and spices. What we drink should follow the same philosophy as what we eat: in our case, fresh, energizing, comforting, and all natural.

This chapter collects some of our favorite juice and smoothie combinations, along with some less common drinks that are part of our family repertoire. Feel free to add a shot of mezcal or rum to any of these!

AGUA FRESCA

Agua fresca, or "fresh water," is less a recipe than it is a concept: The freshest, ripest fruit (as well as the occasional vegetable, flower, nut, or grain) gets blended with water to make it into an all-natural beverage. Aguas frescas are not as concentrated as juices or smoothies, because of the water, but they are far more flavorful and nutritious than store-bought flavored waters.

The quantities in this basic recipe will change based on your personal preference as well as the fruit's sweetness and texture (fruits with higher water content like watermelon or strawberries require less added water, for example, while lower-water-content fruits like mangoes or cherries need more). Some people like to strain the mixture quickly through a fine-mesh strainer to make the agua fresca lighter and clearer, while others want the fiber and other nutrition in the fruit pulp. Lime juice tends to "perk up" fruit in the same way that salt amps up the flavor of savory dishes, but it's optional, especially if the fruit already has a natural tartness. If you feel the fruit requires sugar to augment its flavor, we like the purity of cane sugar, which doesn't contribute any real flavor of its own, but feel free to use any sweetener you like.

In a blender, add the fruit, 1 cup water, sugar (start with very little, if any, since you can add more later), and lime juice, if using. Blend on high speed for at least a full minute to completely liquefy the fruit. If the fruit has seeds, like most berries or passion fruit, you may want to strain it. Serve over ice in a large glass or mason jar.

SERVES 1

1 cup chopped fresh fruit

Cane sugar or other sweetener, to taste

1 tablespoon freshly squeezed lime juice (optional)

TOTAL PREPARATION TIME

15 minutes

CANTALOUPE-SEED HORCHATA
(Horchata de Semilla de Melón)

Most people know horchata as a creamy drink made exclusively from rice, but in some parts of Mexico it's made with oats, barley, nuts, or seeds. Much like the Jalapeño-Egg Fritter (page 104), this recipe is a great zero-waste use of something that's usually thrown away. There's no need to clean the pulp from cantaloupe seeds, since the pulp has flavor, too. Seeds from honeydew melon can be used here as well.

1. In a medium bowl, add the rice with just enough water to cover it completely. Soak for at least 1 hour. In a blender, add the rice and soaking liquid, along with the cantaloupe seeds and sugar. Blend on high speed until completely smooth, 2 to 4 minutes. Taste the mixture and add more sugar, if desired. Strain through a fine-mesh strainer lined with cheesecloth and discard the solids.

2. Pour into a pitcher and stir in about 8 cups water (you may prefer more or less, depending on personal taste). Serve over ice, garnished with the pecans and grapefruit.

SERVES 6 TO 8

2 cups long-grain white rice

1 cup cantaloupe seeds

¾ cup sugar

2 tablespoons chopped pecans

1 grapefruit, peel and pith removed, diced and seeded

TOTAL PREPARATION TIME

15 minutes, plus 1 hour soaking time

MEXICAN FRUIT PUNCH
(Ponche de Frutas)

Traditionally, this drink is served during Christmas in Mexico, and when we came to the US, we wanted to pass down some of these traditions to our younger family members. In December, we'd gather at my brother's house and build a fire for the decoratively glazed clay ponche pot. Each niece and nephew had an ingredient they were responsible for, and when our mom would call out the ingredient, each kid would happily throw it into the pot. Once all the ingredients were incorporated, we would sit around the fire, talk, laugh, reminisce, and wait for the sweet smell of the sugar cane and piloncillo to alert us that it was ready. Goya Ponche en Almíbar is a combination of pineapple, sugar cane, and tejocotes (a Mexican fruit) in a cinnamon-sugar syrup. It's easy to find in Mexican markets, especially around the holidays. It's something we always put in ponche as kids, so it's part of our tradition, and it adds another layer of comforting flavor.

In a large stockpot, combine 3 quarts water, the guavas, sugar, and canela and bring to a boil over high heat. Once the mixture has boiled for 10 minutes, add the pears, apples, oranges, pineapple, prunes, and raisins and cook for another 10 minutes. Add the jar of ponche, including the syrup, with 4 cups water, and heat through. Taste and add more sugar to sweeten or more water to make it less sweet. Serve hot or warm. Ponche keeps in the refrigerator for about 3 days; reheat before serving.

SERVES 12

6 guavas, quartered

1 cup packed dark brown sugar

2 canela sticks (Mexican, or Ceylon, cinnamon)

2 pears, cored and diced

2 apples, cored and diced

3 oranges, peeled and diced

1 cup fresh pineapple chunks

10 prunes

½ cup raisins, black or golden

One 32-ounce jar Goya-brand Ponche en Almíbar (fruit punch)

TOTAL COOK TIME

45 minutes

HOT PINEAPPLE-CORN DRINK
(Atole de Piña)

Veracruz produces 65 percent of Mexico's pineapples, far more than any other state. We might be biased, but Veracruz pineapples are the best in Mexico. When Mamá Reyna was fourteen, her first job was in a pineapple-processing plant. She had to clean and peel the pineapple completely—no rind, nothing on there but that bright yellow. The pineapples would be piled on long tables, and she had to be fast and efficient to get through them all. She was so good that they moved her up to pineapple packaging, which was a more desirable position. She says this recipe not only reminds her of that job, but of her father, who would request it to cure his hangovers (we don't know why, but it seems to work!). In turn, it makes us think of our abuelito as well.

SERVES 8 TO 12

3 sticks canela (Mexican, or Ceylon, cinnamon)

1 (2-pound) very ripe fresh pineapple, peeled, cored, and chopped

1 cup masa harina, such as Maseca brand

1½ cups sugar, or to taste

TOTAL COOK TIME

30 minutes

1. In a large stockpot, add 16 cups water and the canela. Bring to a simmer over medium heat and let it simmer for 5 minutes. Meanwhile, in a blender, add the pineapple with 2 cups water (in batches, if needed, depending on the size of your blender). Blend until smooth. Pour half of the pineapple mixture through a fine-mesh strainer into the pot, pushing on the solids to get all the liquid out, then dispose of the solids. Pour the other half of the pineapple mixture in the pot as is (that is, if you want some of the fibrous pineapple solids, but not all).

2. Turn the heat down to low. In a medium bowl, whisk the masa harina with 2 cups water until smooth. Slowly whisk the masa into the pot, making sure it doesn't clump as you mix it in. Start adding sugar slowly, tasting as each addition dissolves, until you reach your desired level of sweetness.

3. Turn the heat up to medium and cook, whisking often to avoid the masa clumping or sticking, until it's smooth, silky, and roughly the consistency of heavy cream, 10 to 20 minutes. Remove the canela and serve hot. Garnish with additional canela sticks or pineapple wedges, if desired.

SMOOTHIES

Believe it or not, there are people who come to Veracruz All Natural and just order smoothies and juices—no tacos! These are three of our favorites.

"LA REINA" SMOOTHIE

It's hard to argue with the sweet perfection of this fruit salad in a glass. You can freeze your own berries, or you can use store-bought organic frozen berries with no additional ingredients. There are many mixed-berry blends out there, and one and a half cups of any frozen berry mix will work here. The freshly squeezed juice in this recipe is what really makes it stand apart.

In a blender, puree everything until smooth. Add a little water to adjust the thickness, as desired.

SERVES 2

1 cup frozen strawberries

1 cup freshly squeezed orange juice

1 small ripe banana

¼ cup frozen blueberries

¼ cup frozen raspberries

TOTAL PREPARATION TIME

15 minutes

"LA LEY" SMOOTHIE

SERVES 2

2 cups frozen mango chunks

2 cups fresh spinach

1 cup almond milk or milk of your choice

4 teaspoons peanut butter

1 medium ripe banana

4 teaspoons hemp powder or other protein powder (optional)

TOTAL PREPARATION TIME

15 minutes

This is one of our favorite smoothies to have for breakfast or as an afternoon snack. It's named after our mom, whose nickname is "La Ley" (The Law). You can use store-bought frozen mango chunks or freeze them yourself.

In a blender, puree everything (including the hemp powder, if using) until smooth. Add more milk to adjust the thickness, as desired.

"GOOD MORNING" SMOOTHIE

This is such a simple but delicious combination that gives you a lot of energy in the morning. Pureeing—rather than juicing—the carrots makes this smoothie a great source of fiber.

In a blender, puree everything until smooth; you will puree longer than usual to break down all the carrot fibers.

SERVES 2

1 (1 x 2-inch) piece ginger, peeled

3 medium carrots, peeled and cut into chunks

1½ cups freshly squeezed orange juice

1 cup ice cubes

TOTAL PREPARATION TIME

15 minutes

ACKNOWLEDGMENTS

WE WANT TO EXPRESS OUR deepest gratitude to all the people who participated in making this book.

To our mom, **"La Ley,"** thank you for shaping us into the women, entrepreneurs, and human beings we are today. Through your example you showed us not just what it means to be a mother, but also everything about what it means to be a successful and *chingona* woman. Your most precious gifts—your experience, your knowledge, and your recipes—have inspired this book. It's an honor to share them here, in a collection that is more than a cookbook; it's a celebration of life, legacy, and love. Fulfilling this dream that is as much yours as it is ours is a privilege beyond words. Thank you for your unwavering support—not just as our mom but also as a friend and mentor.

To Lydie Joly de Trejo, **"La Güera,"** thank you for contributing your grain of sand to everything you could in a project that means so much to us. You've become more than a friend; you've truly become a sister. Thank you for showing us what it means to be a good person and for always seeing the light in everything. This experience would not have been the same without your sharp eye as a reader, your voice as a writer, and your artistic soul.

To the best right-hand man anyone could wish for, **Gustavo Moreno**. We will forever be grateful for your hard work and genuine dedication in making this special project a success. We cannot imagine having created this book without you. We're lucky to have you as part of our team.

To Lis-ek Mariscal, **"Lis,"** when we decided to move forward with this project, we had no idea what writing a cookbook actually entailed. Thank you for being there every step of the way, not just as our communicator and project manager but also as the one who took our thoughts and voices and brought them to life on the page. No one could have done it better than you—you know our story and have walked with us through our hardest moments and happiest milestones. It fills us with joy to know that you'll continue carrying our vision forward. This is a legacy your grandmother passed on to us, and now we're passing it on to you—to protect, to honor, and to keep alive.

To Kitty Cowles, for her support and loyalty, for navigating us through the daunting process of writing a book and for believing that our story and our food could have wide appeal.

To Doris Cooper and Maria Espinosa, for giving this book such focused attention and lending critical eyes while honoring our voices and our food.

Special thanks to our photography team: photographer and director Mackenzie Smith, food stylist Maite Aizpurua, prop stylist Audrey Davis, Ben Mistak, Robert Amador, and Andrew Runkle.

Maritza would like to thank her husband, Corey: Thank you for being my constant source of emotional support. You are my biggest cheerleader, and I know I can always count on you to have my back in everything I do. Your belief in me inspires me to keep growing and striving to be the best version of myself. I love you, honey. Thank you for being by my side and making me laugh when I need it the most.

To all those who contributed their *granito de arena*, have helped support our dreams, and to the city of Austin for embracing us and our food with open arms.

INDEX

ABOUT THE AUTHORS

REYNA AND MARITZA VÁZQUEZ ARE SISTERS. Shortly after crossing the Mexico–Texas border, they put everything they had into a tiny food truck. Today, they live in Austin, where they are nationally renowned for serving some of the best Mexican and Mexican American food in the country. They have seven outposts of their taquería, Veracruz All Natural; a restaurant, Veracruz Fonda and Bar, which won a Michelin Bib Gourmand; and a mezcalería, La Mezca. Born in Veracruz, Mexico, Reyna and Maritza have been featured in *The New York Times*, the *Los Angeles Times*, *Rolling Stone*, Food Network, and more.